CW00429494

BFI TV Classics

BFI TV Classics is a series of books celebrating key individual television programmes and series. Television scholars, critics and novelists provide critical readings underpinned with careful research, alongside a personal response to the programme and a case for its 'classic' status.

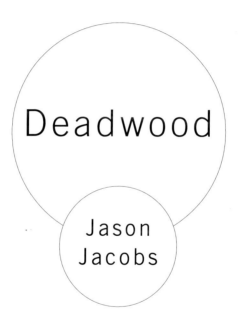

Deadwood

Jason
Jacobs

A BFI book published by Palgrave Macmillan

For Steven Peacock
Sláinte

First published in 2012 by
PALGRAVE MACMILLAN

on behalf of the

BRITISH FILM INSTITUTE
21 Stephen Street, London W1T 1LN
www.bfi.org.uk

There's more to discover about film and television through the BFI. Our world-renowned archive, cinemas, festivals, films, publications and learning resources are here to inspire you.

Palgrave Macmillan in the UK is an imprint of Macmillan Publishers Limited, registered in England, company number 785998, of Houndmills, Basingstoke, Hampshire RG21 6XS. Palgrave Macmillan in the US is a division of St Martin's Press LLC, 175 Fifth Avenue, New York, NY 10010. Palgrave Macmillan is the global academic imprint of the above companies and has companies and representatives throughout the world. Palgrave® and Macmillan® are registered trademarks in the United States, the United Kingdom, Europe and other countries.

Set by Cambrian Typesetters, Camberley, Surrey
Printed in China

This book is printed on paper suitable for recycling and made from fully managed and sustained forest sources. Logging, pulping and manufacturing processes are expected to conform to the environmental regulations of the country of origin.

British Library Cataloguing-in-Publication Data
A catalogue record for this book is available from the British Library
A catalog record for this book is available from the Library of Congress
10 9 8 7 6 5 4 3 2 1
21 20 19 18 17 16 15 14 13 12

ISBN 978–1–84457–362–2

Contents

Acknowledgments

My first thanks goes to Ted Mann who was eager to talk with me about his writing for *Deadwood* and instrumental in allowing me to visit Red Board Productions in Santa Monica in March 2010. There, David Milch was extremely patient and generous, allowing me access to the scripts and other materials relating to the production of the show. Scott Willson also made me very welcome, and Bill Clark was generous too in the expansiveness of his conversation. While this book lays a lot of emphasis on the creative centrality of David Milch, he would be the first to acknowledge that *Deadwood* is absolutely the product of collaboration and I apologise to the creative personnel who may have received little or no mention here.

This book was written with the support of the Cultural History Project funded by the Faculty of Arts at the University of Queensland. Thanks to my friend Alison Taylor who was there at the start, and to Val, Henry, Hannah and Laura who had to put up with the early morning sound of the show for years, and much more besides. I am grateful to Bill Rothman for his wonderful words and for alerting me to the poetry of *Justified*. Finally, thanks to Steven Peacock who was its first reader and whose response encouraged me to keep faith when all seemed lost.

1 Arriving in Deadwood

The opening shot of the pilot 'Deadwood' is sparse and unpromising.
After a lively credit sequence, we fade up to a deserted dirt street in a
Western town at night; there is a saloon, but it is quiet; centrally in the
frame is a simple scaffold. At the end of the street, a horse and rider
wander apparently without purpose and the camera pans with them
past what we now recognise as a gallows to reveal another building, one
with bars on its window – a jailhouse. A caption tells us this is 'Montana
Territory, May 1876' but the town's name is not written; despite the
generically familiar iconography – horse and rider, wooden buildings of
a certain architectural style – it is all something of a blank, a sketch of a
place like an empty stage or a vacant movie set waiting for its action to
begin. The next shot comes from inside the jailhouse and marks a
hesitation. We see a pen freshly dipped in an iron inkpot being taken by
strong hand to paper; we hear but do not see the blunt scratch of writing
as the camera rises to reveal the pen's master, Marshal Seth Bullock
(Timothy Olyphant). He stops, pausing for thought; or, perhaps, having
written the date, time and place he is waiting, like us, to begin.
Everything that follows from this pausing rewrites not only the Western
genre but our imagination of the possibilities and artistic range of
television fiction; from this moment of still and rest onwards, we are
cast headlong into *Deadwood*, a vivid, filthy, world in motion, a violent
destabilising of our expectations of television drama in language,
incident and character. In minutes, Bullock will no longer be a lawman
and will leave this settled, still place after executing the solitary prisoner

A world brought into view

he holds in his cell. What we think of the historical American West, of the Western as a genre, of the possibilities of television itself will be radically recalibrated. As Bullock pauses with his pen, we know that he is thinking – although we can't know of what – and in the shift of focus that brings into view the prisoner watching in the background, an entire world begins to be defined. That gesture or motion of the camera is the stylistic visual tipping point which begins the momentum of this world: it is *Deadwood*'s *primum movens*.

Bullock is alive and attentive to words and their troublesome claims on meaning and this is not the last time in the show we see him stuck. In the first episode of the third season, he asks his wife Martha (Anna Gunn) to assist him in writing his election speech since the words in his draft are 'doing the wrong jobs, piling on too heavy, or at odds over meaning'. That primal sense of contradiction in a thing as basic as a word is also true of Bullock himself and it is telling that in our first look at him, he is in conflict with his own expression. Out of all of *Deadwood*'s extraordinary characters, he is probably the closest to the laconic Western hero familiar to us from decades of movie and television serials. Like them, he chooses his words carefully and is good at violence.

But we don't see what he writes: instead the world behind him is brought into clarity (the technique is called 'racking focus' and will become the show's most prominent stylistic signature) – we see a prisoner in the cells, a young man watching him. This is Clell Watson (James Parks) and he owns the show's first spoken words:

> WATSON: Is that some sort of a letter, Marshal?
> BULLOCK: Journal.
> WATSON: Journal? Good.

While not exactly disdainful, Watson's 'good' carries a register of condescension: why would anyone, except an old man in reminiscence or a young girl recording romantic impressions bother to write in a journal? Or perhaps: 'Good – here is a man of thought and imagination. One, therefore, susceptible to reflection and fancy – perhaps I may plant some suggestions of my own …'. Watson's métier, as we shall discover, is language as it is spoken and performed, using words as tools that dig into the world and sink roots into it. As played in a brilliant, all-too-brief cameo by James Parks, the character has a winning charm redolent of Carette's Marceau in *La Règle du jeu* (1939), whose roguish aspect speaks to the hustler and opportunist operating on the energy we'd all like the confidence to exploit occasionally. Parks's performance here is compelling and we need to like him very much so that when he is suddenly taken away we feel the loss keenly. Despite the fact that he shot Bullock in the shoulder as he was apprehended for cattle rustling, Watson still manages to charm him with his lightly gravelled voice and strategically self-pitying patter. We want to listen to him as he entangles Bullock in conversation about his move to the Gold Rush town of Deadwood. Hence, Watson's dramatic function is also to provide exegesis, to convey as well as embody – not least because of his present confinement – the attraction of Deadwood.

3

> WATSON: *No* law at all in Deadwood … is that true?
> BULLOCK: Being on Indian land.

WATSON: So then you won't be a Marshal?
BULLOCK: Taking goods there to open a hardware business, me and my
partner. *[He gets up, begins to pour coffee.]*
WATSON: If I'd've got there I'd've been prospectin'. Jesus *Christ* Almighty.
No law at all. Gold you can scoop from the streams with your bare hands.
And I gotta go fuck myself up by supposedly stealing Byron Sampson's
horse.

We get tight and efficient exposition here with Watson's sense of
wonder at the prospect of lawless freedom given emphasis by the visual
insistence on his present confinement behind bars. They are the
material expression of the Law's authority but, as Watson clearly
realises, it is Bullock's will, *his choice* to enforce that Law that keeps
them locked. And given his decision to quit for a new life altogether,
Watson can taste the possibility that a nudge from a repentant harmless
petty thief might loosen the Marshal's grip on the cell key. After all gold
is real – you can feel it in your palms as you lift it from the mountain
streams – whereas the Law is an abstraction, given material force only
by the buildings and actions of men. Yes, the Law, like God, is an
abstraction – but so are stories: the narratives and fictions we can spin
and craft and which like oars or wings may propel us through the social
world and which act upon it as surely as the Law 'builds' jailhouses and
God churches.

And we see Watson's words doing their work on Bullock;
how the amiable nature of the conversation has created action and
movement; they have taken Bullock away from his journal and
brought him into the social world of conversation and companionship. He pours and brings Watson some coffee as they talk and it
is a measure of the success of the charm offensive that the normally
irascible Bullock is good-humoured about the wound to his
shoulder.

WATSON: I'm sorry as hell about your shoulder.
BULLOCK: Flesh wound. Don't look like it wants to infect.

> WATSON: *[emboldened by the absence of grudge]* Well never mind flesh wounds, Sir. When you are going to meet your maker, you don't feature telling Him that you shot a Marshal in the shoulder for only doing his legally ordained job.
> BULLOCK: He may have heard worse stories.
> WATSON: God? Well if he ain't I'll tell him six – or seven – just on people of my own acquaintance.

Watson is careful in this banter to remind Bullock that his job is 'legally ordained' and different in theory from the world of divine morality. But Watson's confidence – he's more or less claiming he has the ability to charm the Almighty with his tales – is desperately needed since we must now realise what 'going to meet your maker' might mean. Together with the scaffold outside, it adds up to the fact that Watson is condemned to death and Bullock is his guard and executioner. These are ultimate stakes and Watson is talking not just for freedom but for his life. Escape is tantalisingly close and he needs only to persuade this man who in hours will no longer be a Marshal and therefore whose commitment to enforcing the Law that executes those who steal from the rich and powerful is, given his destination of the lawless town of Deadwood, reasonably in doubt. Judging the moment right, he makes his pitch:

5

> WATSON: I'd like to suggest an idea to you, Sir, that I pray as a Christian man you entertain on its own fucking merits.

Read that line aloud and enjoy its musicality and the kick of the sudden juxtaposition of the sacred and profane. If there was ever a show that animates the flesh and soul of its actors, it is this one: Parks simply delights in the apparent contradiction between the line's early formal rectitude 'pray … Christian … entertain' that are like the coils of a spring released in its later coarseness so we get a sense of the words' dynamism and energy generating but also driving against their own contexts, rhythms and force. There is a whole world, a whole life, in its music, and it is a new fresh language, a new world.

BULLOCK: *[gets up, considers him]* Does it involve letting you go?

WATSON: I know two scores Mr Bullock we could make in transit without going twenty feet off our path, people with cash on hand. And if once we hit Deadwood you didn't want to have to do with me, we'd never speak again, we'd meet as strangers the rest of our fucking lives. Now, what do you think of that?

Perhaps it is fitting that Watson concludes his pitch with a gesture toward a future fictional life where they pretend not to know each other, but the promise of silence from a man whose currency is words is a misjudgement, and that mistake makes us like him even more. For a moment, we might also think Bullock is tempted, but they are interrupted by Sol Star (John Hawkes), Bullock's business partner bringing grim news. The cattle baron Byron Sampson (Christopher Garga) is outside with a liquored-up mob of his cowboys – they've come to torture and kill Watson right now. We seem to be in familiar generic territory for a moment: a jail under siege from brutish elements without who want to usurp the course of the Law for the sake of blood and in doing so threaten the stability and integrity of civil society. So we might expect that the Lawman inside and his allies will do the right thing and defend with their lives the vulnerable criminals for they are good men with forgiveness and justice in their hearts and therefore men fit to cultivate and civilise this land, heroic men who, in William James's phrase can 'stand this life', and whose steady vision provides the gravitational pull and anchor for the labour and industry required to build a better world. And while all of this may be true of Seth Bullock and Sol Star, what happens next is that Clell Watson is hanged by Bullock and left dangling in front of the mob.

The town square which was so bare before is now the stage for a grim spectacle. As we see the baying mob outside replete with flaming torches and led by the fascistic Sampson, Bullock emerges from the jail with Watson wearing a large noose around his neck. Star covers them from a vantage point atop the wagon laden with the hardware goods that they will, in minutes, take with them on their journey to

Deadwood. What follows is a remarkable scene, the first of three in the pilot that seek to orientate *Deadwood*'s audience away from their expectations of the Western genre toward something different. In order to facilitate this move, it has to evoke the genre while pointing to aspects of its 'childishness'. Take the figure of the Lawman. As all 'grown-ups' should know (and the show wants us to understand), police like Bullock are hired by the rich and powerful in order to protect their property and the social order that underpins and naturalises their power. To legitimate such a deal, an abstraction, the Law, is invoked as a supposedly impartial and objective arbiter between interests. Like other cattle barons, Sampson has hired Bullock as Marshal in order to arrest and execute those who steal from him. But Bullock, wearing the emblem of the Law, does not want to give him the satisfaction of making the implicit explicit, and hates the idea of being pushed around by someone he describes as a 'loudmouth cocksucker'. (And, Sampson represents the externalisation of the disordered rage Bullock feels inside: hence his hatred of him):

7

> BULLOCK: I'm executing sentence now and he's hanging under colour of Law … .You called the Law in, Sampson, you don't get to call it off because you're liquored-up and popular on payday.

Watson meanwhile is understandably upset that he's being hanged ahead of schedule ('This ain't right – my sister was coming in the morning'). Instead of using the scaffold, Bullock improvises by throwing the rope over the beam of the jailhouse porch, kicks a stool for Watson to stand on and asks him for his last words to tell his sister. Sampson, seeing events drop away from the grasp of brute force exhorts Watson not to step off the stool.

> WATSON: Or what? You'll kill me?

For viewers, this makes the dramatic issue clear: it is the nature, rather than say the time or place, of his passing that Watson gets to choose, and despite the fact that he is the one about to execute him, he cleaves to Bullock's steadfast and kind authority. Bullock speaks to Watson with civil and strong courtesy, "I'll help you with the drop ... what would you have your sister told?" Hence, we are given a scene where the execution of a man that few viewers could believe actually *deserves* the death sentence is offered as an index of the moral capacity of our leading character. And we see that it is now *Bullock's words* which animate Watson, *his* decency which allows Watson to feel his capacity to 'stand this life' even at the brink of death where, according to the script he discovers 'a feeling ... not as hollow or far from conviction as he'd expected':

> WATSON: Tell my sister if my boy turns up, raise him good.
> BULLOCK: What else?
> WATSON: Tell her. Give him my boots.
> BULLOCK: What else?
> WATSON: Tell him his daddy loved him. *[More confident]* Tell him he asked God's forgiveness.

8

As he speaks, we see another aspect of the power of the spoken word, as a legacy, a narrative patterning of inheritance that is our gift, or curse, to those to whom it is bequeathed: *this is who I was, this is my story*. And in a move that will become typical in *Deadwood*, we see the potent effect such words have on an audience: the mob's excitement is quelled in the face of the spectacle before them and it is quiet, chastened by the authenticity and grace of Watson's final moments, as he steps from the stool after spitting a hearty 'Fuck You!' at Sampson. But, as so often in life, our grandiose plans for a meaningful exit snag along the fabric of grim reality and Watson dangles from the porch choking, slowly strangled by the noose.

This opening scene went through many revisions, and a different version was shot where Watson (played by another actor), is hung on the scaffold in the square, the scene emphasising the painful slowness of his death as Bullock, Sampson and the mob look on. The version that we have makes the crucial change of amplifying the emotional and physical proximity between Bullock and Watson, developing the rapport I've detailed above, and fashioning a situation whereby Bullock, in order to outwit Sampson, improvises the execution on the jailhouse porch. This revision has the effect of framing the final gesture of violence as an intimate thing. As Watson strangles next to him, Bullock's offer to 'help with the drop' is realised – he holds him by the waist and yanks him violently down, snapping his neck. This efficient motion is an early hint of Bullock's capacity for abrupt violence as a response to helplessness.

Now everything is still and quiet save for the dragging of Watson's shoes on the porch; Bullock is writing again, this time fluently with clear purpose. He hands Watson's last words, and his badge, to one of Sampson's chastened men before riding off with his wagon and partner into the night.

* * *

The beginning parts of *Deadwood* are about getting things moving – people, objects, events, storytelling. After Bullock's early hesitation the show gathers momentum, quickly reaching a pitch of activity where nothing – no object, person, word or particle – is at rest. There is a thought in *Deadwood*, associated with the writing process, that becoming 'unblocked' requires not the discovery of a place of rest and reflection, but securing access to and participation in the currents of the social world: the flow and flux of conversation, talk, scheming. The next scene takes the sense of blockage and participation a step further.

It is day and another caption tells us the place is the Black Hills in July 1876, two months after Clell Watson's execution. We see a wagon train – more of a wagon jam – all humans and oxen struggling with wooden wheels in the mud. Inside one of them, an old man lies on a bearskin with his eyes closed, stretched out like a corpse lying in state. He has the long-haired, dandified appearance characteristic of gunslingers depicted in 1990s Westerns such as *Tombstone* (1993) or *Wyatt Earp* (1994) – the 'authentic', revisionist look. The man is Wild Bill Hickok (Keith Carradine) and the dirty face that appears at the

9

hood of the wagon belongs to 'Calamity' Jane Cannary (Robin Weigert) – dressed as a man in buckskin. Biblically hungover, Bill does not open his eyes as they converse about the hold-up: 'Seems like it's tighter out there', he says, 'than a bull's ass in fly season,' a cute metaphor whose vivid colour underscores the theme of crowded migration. Jane admonishes the stuck wagon train in general; she has a rough voice that sounds like it is worn out by constant shouting. 'It's only Wild Bill Hickok you got caught up in the mud', she yells to them, 'you ignorant fucking *cunts*.' The voice carries that word and sounds out all its coarse Anglo-Saxon insult as if well practised in the saying. There will be familiar celebrities in this version of the genre, but they will sound a little different.

Jane pauses in her grumbling to look across the valley down into Deadwood gulch and the camera picks up her gaze and develops it into its own and ours, accompanied by the beginnings of music that evokes movement, wheels turning. Then, in a long shot of the Black Hills, we notice the continuous procession of light canvas wagons moving toward the brown smudge of wooden buildings – a town.

And suddenly we have arrived in Deadwood, riding now with Bullock as he guides his wagon down the main street and takes in the

Bullock sees a world being built

rush of life and labour that hits his eyes. In the way they show slices of mining-camp activity, these shots recapitulate the show's stunning credit sequence. Bullock sees a place in motion, in construction, the sight of humans making their world in all its coarse dynamism. It is Bullock's own 'title sequence' and he is hooked by this spectacle of frenetic commerce created by men seeking their fortunes in the crust of the earth; or like Bullock himself, seeking income by selling equipment, food, sex, alcohol and drugs to those hoping to strike it rich. The music continues that sense of motion but the visuals, now filtered through Bullock's perception, lend it additional resonance; we feel in its repetition and rhythms and melody a sense not only of wheels turning, but of the earth as an industrial mechanism, a revolving sphere to be mastered and mined. The subtle way in which Bullock's moral certainty that he was doing Right, allowed Watson the confidence to discover a final sense of nobility in the face of imminent extinction, finds its mirror here with Bullock once again brought out of himself – out of the mania of his own thoughts – by the vision of Deadwood at work. This theme – of going beyond the self in order to become fully human – is one that *Deadwood* holds dear.

11

It is a reminder of a key force that animates the human race and it has been the job of the Western as a foundation myth to explore such matters as they pertain to America; the appeal of the Western beyond the specificity of American experience points us to its fundamental universalism. Here it is a universalism that starts at a fundamentally base level. David Milch, the creator of *Deadwood*, describes the impact of the news of a gold strike as having the effect of

> suddenly the continent tilts and all the shitbirds roll into the new gold strike … and every misfit who hasn't been able to obey the usual emotional attachments which come with civilised behaviour, they go out there. And here now if you're on Indian land there's no laws at all. So now every shitbird went to Deadwood.[1]

In the Western, the civilising impulse is often under scrutiny and rarely emerges unalloyed; most motives are mixed and in *Deadwood*, while all human action initially seems subordinate to sheer greed, this does not exhaust the impulses and desires that drive it. We have been given a hint that Bullock's own motives may be obscure to him – his hesitation over the journal entry implies that he is inexpressible to himself. And yet he comes to the unstable and unregulated town Deadwood of all places. Why?

Bullock's presence here then seems at first an anomaly, and the chaotic, unregulated scene of human greed at work might seem obnoxious and threatening were it not for the sense that the film style carries of excitement, of variety, of strangers, of new forms of social relations emerging in moments as humanity collides with itself. Perhaps those who crave order are also drawn to the seduction of its chaotic origins. We see buildings being constructed, animals gutted, guns and whisky sold, mining in the street itself, and even a photographer earning his way by sating the desire for record and representation. A teeming mass of humans of various shapes, hairiness and reputation all sharing a single intention: to exploit this environment, to make something of it. The energy depicted here is reminiscent of the young Marx and Engels's description in 'The Communist Manifesto' of the 'uninterrupted disturbance ... everlasting uncertainty of agitation' of the bourgeois epoch:

> All fixed fast-frozen relations, with their train of ancient and venerable prejudices and opinions are swept away, all new formed ones become antiquated before they can ossify. All that is solid melts into air, all that is holy is profaned, and man is at last compelled to face with sober senses his real conditions of life and his relations with his kind.[2]

This passage (apart from the 'sober senses') also captures the aesthetic force of *Deadwood*'s title sequence with its eloquent characterisation of the cosmic liquidity of the planet at the hands of human industry, human desire and sensual experience. It locates the realist specificity – the shapes, costumes and activities – of a nineteenth-century mining town within a visual patterning which stresses their elemental nature (fire,

Elemental flux in *Deadwood*'s title sequence

earth, and – a horse running – wind). All of the textures and processes shown – the butchering tools, the boots, sluices, costumes, shot glasses, etc – are anchored as realistic period detail yet simultaneously convey impressionistic senses of flux, fluidity, transition and change, most obviously in the repeated shots of water and rippling reflections of the material world in it, a sense which culminates in the ultimate emblem of human beauty, a voluptuous woman's dirty body, dipping gracefully into a tin bath. The hand as tool replaces the face as an emblem of anonymous humanity (no characters are featured in the titles); we see them sifting through the sluices, chopping animals, holding cards, touching flesh. These *alivenesses* are socialised. Such fragments are joined by the repeated shots of an unsaddled and riderless horse journeying through what are presumably the woods around the town. It arrives then vanishes in the main street outside the *Gem Saloon*. This skittish emblem of the Western seems strangely excluded from the world, as if it is a spectator rather than participant, an ungrounded symbol. Nonetheless its enigmatic qualities deepen the sense of a genre piece that has travelled decisively into the unknown.

Bullock's arrival in Deadwood recapitulates and domesticates the resonances of the credits and he also models audience awe at the sights of this rowdy agitated spectacle of the town. Like us, he is a new element in town, who we might expect will react explosively to this mob-like environment, badge or no. Somehow Sol Star has arrived ahead of Bullock and found a lot to pitch their shop. 'No construction', says the large man, Dan Dority (W. Earl Brown), who sells them the lease: 'Twenty dollars a day payable every morning to Mr Swearengen at the *Gem*.' If the continent, as Milch contends, is tilted toward the gold strike in Deadwood, then the main road runs like a funnel or urethra to the *Gem*.

* * *

This is a Western about the origins of things – of law, order, civilisation, America, of the way we are as beings in a world of things, and it is therefore appropriate we first see its central character Al Swearengen (Ian McShane), proprietor of the *Gem* – a swarthy Miltonic pimp and it appears in these early episodes that there are no limits to the moral depths which his villainy will plumb in order to maintain and enhance what he calls his 'operation' in the camp – transforming the elemental into money. He is conducting the transaction with Ellsworth (Jim Beaver) a dirt-blasted, hairy miner and the matter between these men is an exchange – the miner has given Swearengen gold, which is weighed and valued in exchange for services provided … at the *Gem*. One thing becomes another, the conversion of a cosmic element for sensual reward: sex, alcohol, the thrill of winning money. Gold is the beautiful emblem of the truth of the being of things since it symbolises the substitutability of objects. According to philosopher George Simmel, author of *The Philosophy of Money*,

> The philosophical significance of money is that it represents within the practical world the most certain image and the clearest embodiment of the formula of all being, according to which things receive their meaning through each other, and have their being determined by mutual relations.[3]

Gold is the antecedent of money, the symbol which has animated this world and our first sight of it is in Swearengen's fist – he knows its weight and its value and his words capture the alchemy of economic transaction:

> SWEARENGEN: Eight ounces of gold for twenty dollars an ounce is a hundred sixty plus ten dollars for a half ounce makes one-seventy total.
> ELLSWORTH: Inform your dealers and whores of my credit and pour me a god dammed drink.

15

Ellsworth's declaration of principles

While the scene appears to be an exchange of one thing for another, we can hardly miss the fact that Swearengen is taking gold in exchange for credit for services he alone will supply; as viewers, we are being taught a historical truth about how mining camps operate. Ellsworth looks as if he's been digging in the earth the entire day whereas Swearengen, the man holding the gold, is washed and dry and groomed. The thought here is that the labour of *extracting gold* continues long after it has been liberated from the rocks, and that Swearengen's business is mining the miners.

Although we do not get to see much of it as a substance in itself, any more than we see very much, with a couple of important exceptions, of the process of mining it, gold is the mute animating force of Deadwood's society. But the *meaning* of gold as a symbol is fluid and ever changing, and *Deadwood*'s artistic experiment is to force the competing and conflicting meanings humans give to their experiences and aspirations into the dramatic petri dish of a historical mining town. Hence, the real generic innovation has little to do with the explicit intensity of its obscenity, nudity and violence, but instead to foreground the economic basis of modern human ontology by giving its central characters' primary roles as shopkeepers, retailers and bankers. When Bullock leaves the anonymous Montana town for Deadwood in order to set up, of all things, something as boring as a *hardware store* selling pots and pans, he is apparently leaving the classic genre confrontation between men of honour and corrupt capitalist evil, and in that movement the show shifts the generic axis of the Western at the same time as it further universalises it.

This universalising gesture is why Ellsworth is not offered to us as merely an exploited worker. Instead, downing his shot he offers a statement of existential exultation with his lot:

ELLSWORTH: I may have fucked my life up flatter than hammered shit but I stand before you today beholden to no human cocksucker and working a paying fuckin' gold claim – and not the US government saying I'm trespassing or the savage fuckin' Red Man himself or any of these

16

limber-dick cocksuckers passing themselves off as prospectors had better
try and stop me.
SWEARENGEN: They better not try it in here.

This declaration of autonomy from state, ethnic threat and immediate
competition is a robust defence of individualism and it provides
redemptive dignity. The idea that heroic individualism breathes life
and creates stature is given strength by the sheer explosive poetry of
Ellsworth's language; part alliterative and borne by the rapid repetition
of long, then short, vowel sounds ('hammered … human … holden …
fucked … sucker'), it carries a savage relentlessness which is its armour.
It is muscular and tough, a protective shield, like a mining hat, required
in order to navigate and protect against the hostile environment. It is a
toughness that allows one to continue socialising without revealing
much about the self or your past. Beginning again in Deadwood means
however much one's life has been 'fucked up', the slate is clean from
here on in. Ellsworth's question to Swearengen – 'with that damn limey
accent, are those rumours true that you're descended from the British
nobility?' is met with the obscenity that does the job of responding while
maintaining anonymity: 'I'm descended from all those *cocksuckers*.'

The unrelenting obscenity of the language also functions to
assault the viewer's tolerances in order to allow them to experience the
danger and uncertainty of the camp viscerally, a tactic further developed
in the next scene where we see that one of Swearengen's whores, Trixie
(Paula Malcomson), has shot a Trick through the temple for beating her.
Somehow he is still alive slumped against the wall and gibbering when
Swearengen and his henchmen Dan Dority and Johnny Burns (Sean
Bridgers) arrive in the small room. He tells Swearengen where to locate
a note in his jacket containing the details of his next of kin; a haggard
and bespectacled medico, Doc Cochran (Brad Dourif) arrives and is, like
us, astonished at the macabre scene, while Burns and Dority react as
audience surrogates, flinching at the gruesome sight of a man trying
to finger his own mortal head wound. As the camera pulls back and up
and the man dies, we get a tableau of the group and another silence in

17

response to the spectacle of death. A brief moment of stillness and all is action again, with Swearengen directing the clean-up operation – clearly this is not the first time he's had to dispose of a corpse. He instructs his men to 'get the Chinaman' and a sled to move the body, a disposal procedure or motif that will run throughout *Deadwood*. 'You drink free tonight … and I'd hope any talk of this would keep the gun from the whore's hand – bastard did himself in,' he tells Cochran, who remains puzzled as to how the Trick stayed alive for twenty minutes shot through the brain. 'Prospect in him', says Swearengen and we see Cochran insert a steel probe straight through the Trick's temple until it pokes out the other side, carrying a lump of gore. This is the visual equivalent of Henry James's 'turn of the screw', ramping up the visceral challenge for the viewer and daring them to continue to watch. Like the use of obscenity, it is a tactic of pushing our sensibilities as strongly as possible in the hope that surviving the onslaught we will bind to the show ever more strongly. This is followed through in what the script describes as a 'counselling session' where Swearengen explains to Trixie – and us – that killing Tricks is 'bad for my business' before nearly strangling her on the floor with his boot on her throat. When Trixie – already bruised and bloody from her beating by the dead Trick – chokes out, 'I'll be good' and is released we realise that not even the discourse of feminism – at least not 'plucky women do it for themselves out West' – will protect us from what we might be exposed to. As an audience, we have to pass these 'tests' of witnessing the morally repugnant execution of Clell Watson, the spectacle of human destruction of the environment and unremitting individualist greed in Deadwood's main street, the ferocity of obscenity in a relentlessly exploitative environment, the obscene shock of witnessing a gory death and para-autopsy, and finally, the savage brutalisation of an already-beaten prostitute. These events all happen in the first act of the pilot and, apart from providing early shadings of character, offer no lasting narrative consequences but they constitute our 'arrival' in *Deadwood* the show. (The rest of the episode includes the Trick being fed to pigs, the stabbing in bed of one of Swearengen's accomplices, and the massacre, dismemberment and eating by wolves of a family with three

Another turn of the screw

children just outside the camp.) If we get through their tough rendering of
violence, obscenity and cruelty we will still find that it is, as the DVD box
set caption tells us it is 'a hell of a place to make your fortune', and a
compelling location we do not want to leave.

19

   As will be clear by the amount of space that I've devoted to
only the first twenty minutes of the show, I am not going to be able to
explore the full range of *Deadwood*'s achievement. It is an achievement
that does not depend, however, on its distance from the traditional
Western. Although I think *Deadwood* does shift the coordinates of the
Western genre, this is not to claim that there was anything 'wrong' with
that genre before *Deadwood* came along; its achievement does not
depend on the negation of what went before. For example, Robert
Pippin's *Hollywood Westerns and American Myth* and Jim Kitses's new
edition of *Horizons West: Directing the Western from John Ford to
Clint Eastwood*, have very different interests and intentions but both
writers devote most of their attention to what might be called the
traditional Western genre, and both demonstrate the richness of many
artworks produced in Hollywood within it.[4]

   If my references tend to come from literature rather than film
or television, this is chiefly because David Milch's background is steeped

in the American literary tradition as well as in his previous work in
television; it is not because I think a 'literary Western' is *ipso facto* more
compelling, or, to endorse Kitses's complaint at the way Eastwood's
Unforgiven was considered good for transcending the genre ('an ancient
insult'),[5] that *Deadwood* lifts up a 'lowly genre'. I think literature is the
main reference point not because the movie Western genre is incapable of
producing art, but rather because the size, range and diversity of over
thirty hours of television fiction in one world has simply no cinematic
equivalent. The case I will make for *Deadwood*'s status as a classic
depends on qualities that it shares with a classic of American literature.
As we shall see, the magisterial multi-volume textbook *American
Literature: The Makers and the Making* was written by David Milch's
colleagues and teachers at Yale, Cleanth Brooks, R. W . B. Lewis and
Robert Penn Warren; Milch himself was their research assistant for the
project. In the section on Herman Melville, the description of *Moby Dick*
as a problem for criticism sets a mood for thinking about *Deadwood*:

> Much too large and various, too crowded with contrasting incidents and
> competing ideas, too rich in metaphor and symbol to be taken account of
> in a relatively brief commentary. For that reason, however, it may be more
> helpful to pause over a few moments characteristic of the diversity of this
> bursting narrative, rather than to attempt an abstract and thus inevitably a
> reductive overall interpretation. By doing so we can give some sense of the
> way Melville establishes his themes and expands upon them ... how he
> thickens the context and deploys his rhetoric[6]

In order to emulate this approach, I've alternated in the chapters that
follow between studies of pairs of characters and more contextual and
thematic matters. There is much that I have left out, not least an account
of the show's belly-ripping comedy which forms so much a part of its
companionship with its viewers. I have tried not to reproduce the
immensely rich insights offered by the published versions of *Deadwood*
such as those found on the DVD/Blu-Ray editions – the documentaries,
features and audio commentaries on episodes by actors, producers and

writers; nor would I want to direct attention away from the fascinating material found in the extraordinary book on the show, *Deadwood: Stories of the Black Hills* or from the essays in David Lavery's edited collection, *Deadwood: A Western to Swear By.*[7] There is also a growing academic interest, from various disciplines, in the show's achievements, signalling that it has outlasted the initial flurry of interest and praise that tends to stalk any new film or television phenomenon. What matters about *Deadwood* as much as its relationship to the contexts or time and place of its making is how it is able, like any good art, to transcend that time and place and continue to speak to us now and in the future.

2 History

Men's memories are uncertain and the past that was differs little from the past that was not.

Judge Holden, in Cormac McCarthy, *Blood Meridian*.

Second chances … fresh starts. It's how the country got settled.

Jimmy Flynn, *Big Apple*.[8]

Our vivid introduction to the brutal world of *Deadwood* in the pilot episode is tied to the experiences of key characters as they too find their feet in the camp for the first time. After paying Al Swearengen for the lot, Bullock and Star set up their hardware store in a tent and begin selling their goods. Soon after, they are visited by Reverend Smith (Ray McKinnon), a kindly, gentle-spoken man, and polite introductions are exchanged:

> BULLOCK: I'm from Etobicocke, Ontario.
> SMITH: So you were born in Canada?
> BULLOCK: I came to Montana when I was seventeen. That's when I met up with Mr Star.
> SMITH: Is that so?
> STAR: I was born in Austria.
> SMITH: Austria! Wonderful where people come from.

All three of these characters are based on real people: Seth Bullock was born in Canada, served as Sheriff in Montana and did indeed single-handedly execute the real Clell Watson. He then went with Sol Star, his Jewish business partner and friend, to set up a hardware store in Deadwood in 1876. Star was eventually to serve as Mayor of that town for ten terms; Bullock became a good friend of Teddy Roosevelt, and led his inauguration parade; the Reverend Henry Weston Smith was the first preacher to serve in the Black Hills and was murdered there by Indians or possibly road agents in the summer of 1876. That these people were real and these events happened anchors the show in the bedrock of historical fact but this only goes so far. There's no record of the above conversation taking place between Smith, Star and Bullock or even that the three of them ever met. Of course, the show does not aim for a documentary reconstruction of events. Instead, its ambition concerns the matter of realistic truth-telling about *its* rather than history's characters, and in order to do that it must depart from strict adherence to the historical facts. So although many of the figures we see dramatised in the show – Al Swearengen, E. B. Farnum, Jack Langrishe, Charlie Utter, A.W. Merrick and George Hearst – have historical referents, the show interprets their biography for its own dramatic purposes. These people although real were not well known before *Deadwood* in the same way that cultural products – Western films, dime novels, songs – had already constructed various characterisations of Wild Bill Hickok and Calamity Jane in the popular imagination, so there are different registers of biographical realism at stake here. As *Deadwood* develops its stories, it uses a combination of sheer invention and interpretation of historical events to create a place that, while it has some grounding in historical reality, is never confined by it. The show is able to use the biographical traces of those figures based on historical individuals as grist for the mill in character development in the service of a larger artistic design. At the same time, they share the fictional world with pure inventions: Alma Garret (Molly Parker), the rich widow from the East resembles a literary creation straight out of Henry James; Doc Cochran is an alloy of two real historical figures, neither of whom set foot in America, let alone Deadwood; Francis Wolcott is an invention, since mining

23

magnate George Hearst's actual agent in the town was a man named Kellogg. And while the 'Nigger General' Samuel Fields was a real larger-than-life historical presence in the town, whatever reality he had is displaced by Franklyn Ajaye's absorbing performance. *Deadwood* takes the raw facts of history – say, that Ellis Albert Swearengen (1845–1904) from Oskaloosa, Iowa owned a notorious brothel in Deadwood called the *Gem Theatre* – and cooks them up in its larger ambition of discovering what truths such fictional characters in their actions, interactions, thinking and speech, might discover or illuminate. These truths are calibrated not to represent the reality of North America in the 1870s, but to subordinate the depiction of the past in relation to the shifting artistic and dramatic demands of the fictional work in the present, and the reality-dimension of that history adds a particular kind of potency to the fiction. As Donald Sassoon observes in his chapter on Walter Scott in *The Culture of the Europeans*,

24

> The popularity of the historical drama – Shakespeare, Racine and Schiller are names who stand above so many – showed that there was a keen audience for fictionalised history. Myths and epics too dealt with the past. Much of the Bible purports to be 'history'. More generally the structure of most narratives implies that what is being told is an event that has taken place at some time other than the present. History – loosely defined – was always of interest.[9]

Scott's novels often stage the collision between modernity and the wild and lawless that is so central to *Deadwood* and the American Western in general. The important creative difficulty is in judging how to use the authority of historical substance and detail in a way that enhances rather than compromises the drama of the fictional world. This is not a simple matter, like a recipe or a formula and, as we shall see, *Deadwood*'s relationship to the historical Deadwood is a complex matter not least because the show is interested not only in the origins of contemporary America in the savagery of the West – a fairly worn-out theme mined by many Westerns – but in thinking about *origin* – say, the source and nature of human identity, solidarity, impulse, desire, violence and order – by dramatising the connections between the details of objective circumstances and the actions of its characters. To explore such matters, the show anchors itself in cosmic bedrock: the formation and discovery of a fundamental element, gold, and the symbolic meanings that accrue to it.

Deadwood begins with the fact of the Gold Rush of 1876. According to Milch, "There's gold in them thar hills!" refers to the Black Hills of South Dakota, a mountain range in the vast land region west of the Mississippi called the Great Plains. Rising like a target in concentric circles around a central granite dome, the Black Hills are the only remaining exposed feature of an immense thickening of the earth's crust which occurred two billion years ago and which was integral to the formation of the North American continent.[10] Many of the oldest rocks on the planet can be found there and its geological pedigree offers some of the richest ores in the world: not only the estimated 55 million ounces of gold which were eventually extracted from the region, but deposits of lithium, tantalum, beryllium and uranium – all of which became vital during the equipping of the vast US military during the World Wars of the twentieth century. The Lakota Sioux, who conquered the region from the Cheyenne in the eighteenth century, consider the Hills to be the *axis mundi* – the centre of the world.

An early cut of the pilot emphasises this cosmic dimension by beginning with a voiceover narration from Sol Star as we see alternating still black-and-white images of Deadwood's main street and some of its characters:

Maybe we was just a dream the hills dreamed. Maybe the hills was dreamin' us before we ever got to 'em so they'd have something to watch until it was time to get turned upside down again by whatever made the earth and stars or blowed up by a comet or the wind and water worn back to nothing. Maybe we was just the hills' entertainment. If that was it, we showed them a hell of a damn time.

The Fort Laramie Treaty of 1868 confirmed title of the Hills to the Sioux and this is what Bullock means when he says to Watson that Deadwood has no law 'being on Indian land'. But gold is the solvent of treaties with Native Americans, especially in times of national crisis. In the mid-1870s, America was in the Reconstruction Era, still living in the shadow of the Civil War and struggling through what was to become a decade-long depression initiated by a financial panic in 1873. According to Shelby Foote, 'the Civil War defined us as what we are and it opened us to being what we became … . It was the crossroads of our being.'[11] For Robert Pippin, the war

> reminds us that with the failure, in effect, of our first attempt to form and sustain a new type of national unity we needed to hope for a national reconciliation – a 'problem' of human spirit not simply a problem of practical reason. We receive in many Westerns not just a mythic account of the founding of legal, civil society, with an American inflection, but the expression of a great anxiety about what this particular founded society will be like, whether it can hold together, whether it can really leave behind what it was. By this I mean leaving behind the mythic and largely feudal notion of nearly complete self-sufficiency and self-reliance, an honour code, the unavoidability of violence in establishing and maintaining proper status and order, a largely male and isolated world. … If we treat Westerns as a reflection on the possibility of modern bourgeois domestic societies to sustain themselves, command allegiance and sacrifice, defend themselves from enemies, inspire admiration and loyalty … then one surprising aspect of many Westerns … is a profound doubt about the ability of modern societies … to do just that.[12]

Hence, *Deadwood* is set in a period of profound uncertainty and crisis which allows it to meditate on the nature of settlement and its relationship to contemporary society. It is a settlement which begins with the insufficiently harnessed ambitions of ego and vanity.

A veteran of the Civil War, by the time he arrived in the Black Hills in 1874, Lt Col George Custer had already been fighting in the

Indian wars for nearly a decade. He was eagerly responsive to the pull – real or imagined – of the national need for uplift, as well as to his own aspirations for fame, status and celebrity. In the summer of 1874, he was ordered by the US government to lead an expeditionary force to the Black Hills which were, according to him, 'as yet unseen by human eyes except those of Indians', in order to scout a suitable location for a fort.[13] This expedition caused the Gold Rush, which antagonised the Sioux, eventually provoking the war which cost Custer his life at the Battle of Little Bighorn. He was an effective manipulator of the media and, knowing about the rumours of gold deposits in the region that had been around for decades (begun by a Roman Catholic missionary, Father De Smet), Custer insisted on bringing a geologist to accompany the expedition; this was taken by the press and eventually the wider public to mean that Custer was leading a state-backed gold hunt. According to one historian, 'as Custer left the fort, with a pack of reporters and an official photographer in tow, he carried with him the heady hope of his nation for a new bonanza of private fortunes and national wealth'.[14] He also brought along the 7th Cavalry, including three Gatling guns and 1,000 soldiers.

27

By all accounts, the expedition found beautiful country but in July they also discovered gold and news of this – inflated by Custer's assertion (echoed by Clell Watson) that the gold was 'found … in the roots of the grass … at the expense of but little time or labour' – meant that soon thousands began to flood into the area and the Rush began, making the camps and settlements of what would become Custer, Lead and Deadwood frontier boomtowns ripe with gold, money and lawlessness. As a result, the Fort Laramie Treaty had to face the stark reality of Manifest Destiny; as the *Bismarck Tribune* trumpeted: 'The American people need the country the Indians now occupy; many of our people are out of employment; the masses need some new excitement …'.[15] This sentiment is echoed in the little speech A. W. Merrick (Jeffrey Jones), Deadwood's sole journalist and editor of the *Deadwood Pioneer*, makes to the crowd in Tom Nuttall's (Leon Rippy) bar shortly after Hickok and Charlie Utter (Dayton Callie) arrive there: it effectively sets out the political stakes which will occupy *Deadwood*'s three seasons:

> MERRICK: The paradox is the massacre at Little Bighorn signalled the Indians' death throes, Mr Utter. History has overtaken the Treaty which gave them this land – well, the gold we found has overtaken it. I believe within a year Congress will rescind the Fort Laramie Treaty. Deadwood and these hills will be annexed to the Dakota Territory and we who have pursued our destiny outside law or statute will be restored to the bosom of the nation![16]

By June 1875, reports of wider gold finds and the availability of agricultural land to support a mining population further boosted the Rush, as did other expeditions which confirmed the mineral value of the area. Like a giant magnet, this attracted thousands of Americans – amateur and professional miners, obviously, but also entrepreneurs looking to exploit the sudden massing and concentration of humanity in one area; last-chance criminals and hustlers working angles, all of them looking for a fresh start, new opportunities; in a microcosm, it was America beginning again. Economic migration is a fundamental expression of aspiration as well as, for some, desperation. Banking on striking lucky betrays intolerance for the regularity of purpose and industry exemplified in the life and writings of America's founding fathers. But, if you've fucked your life up flatter than hammered shit, this was the place to come for a new start. Despite standing orders to enforce the Treaty and expel the growing number of miners, the US Army troops in the area, led by General George Crook, were reluctant to be harsh; most were sympathetic and many soldiers deserted in order to prospect. By 1876, President Ulysses S. Grant had instructed the military to lay off the miners and the Great Sioux War was well underway.

When we see Bullock and Star leave Montana, it is May 1876 and by the time they arrive in the town, it is July: between those dates (on 25 June or thereabouts) Custer was defeated and killed by Sioux warriors led by the courageous Crazy Horse at the Battle of Little Bighorn, an event that sealed forever the fate of the Sioux in that region. As with Merrick's speech, a lot of this history filters through to us in dialogue exchanges between characters. For example, in outlining his history in the camp to his newly arrived rival *Bella Union* saloon owner Cy Tolliver (Powers Boothe), Swearengen's patter also functions as historical exposition:

> SWEARENGEN: I was here last year too. But the fucking cavalry drove us out.
> TOLLIVER: Put all the whites out didn't they?
> SWEARENGEN: O, deep fucking thinkers in Washington put forward that policy. This year though, so many soldiers deserting to prospect, gave up the ghost, let us all back in. And of course, Custer sorted out the fuckin' Sioux for us, so now we're all as safe as at our mother's tits.
> TOLLIVER: Did a job for our side didn't he Al?
> SWEARENGEN: How about that long-haired fuckin' blowhard, huh? I'll tell you this son, you mark my words. Crazy Horse winning that Little Bighorn bought his people one good long-term ass-fucking. You do not want to be a dirt-worshipping heathen from this fuckin' point forward.[17]
>
> ('Reconnoitring the Rim')

Deadwood is based in this historical reality and the characters, look and broad structure of its stories are tied to that history, so that we know that the main events of the first season take place between July and September 1876, while the second season occurs in 1877, with the third and final one taking place roughly six weeks later. The busyness of the camp and the constant stream of arrivals provides a useful structuring mechanism throughout, allowing new characters and narrative complications to literally arrive on the stage into town: Cy Tolliver and his *Bella Union* crew, Seth Bullock's wife and son, George Hearst's (Gerald McRaney) geologist Francis Wolcott (Garret Dillahunt)and then Hearst himself; Jack Langrishe (Brian Cox) and his theatre company. Occasionally, it is possible to anchor specific events in Deadwood to historical ones, so that when Red Cloud and Spotted Tail were coerced into signing a peace treaty on 7 September 1876 we hear about it as the posse sent to get vaccine for the smallpox plague (also a real event) returns to the camp ('Suffer the Little Children'). But *Deadwood* is careful never to be hostage to history; indeed, like many revisionist Westerns, it is interested in the very nature of history as a 'lie agreed upon'.[18] Sometimes, the distance between the public inscription of history and the darker reality behind it, is dramatised for us. In the final episode of season one 'Sold under Sin', Gen Crook (Peter Coyote) rides his cavalry into camp shortly after defeating the Miniconjou Sioux at the Battle of Slim Buttes (10 September 1876). At Swearengen's request, they hold a parade in the main street where Crook makes a speech to the assembled crowd; here a public performance which constructs a historical narrative is set against the enervating reality of individual experience. As Bullock listens to Crook's speech, a ragged, scarred and lice-ridden soldier standing next to him offers a *sotto voce* revisionist 'authentic' commentary:

> CROOK: The Sioux and Cheyenne, having burned the prairie to deny us fodder for our mounts. Our provisions limited to what we could carry. We turned to the Black Hills when the rains began.
> SOLDIER: Where my bay mare Sheridan she foundered and he had her shot.
> CROOK: That march through mud was a trial sent by God. And harsh necessity required of us much suffering and great sacrifice.
> SOLDIER: Ate our fuckin' horses.
> CROOK: Continuing south we proved our worth against the Indian. We came upon a village at Slim Buttes and at once attacked from all four sides. Their resistance was overcome. There were no prisoners.
> SOLDIER: Paid 'em out. Man, woman and child for my have'n eaten my mare. ('Sold under Sin')

We not only see the discrepancy between Crook's subtle elision – 'There were no prisoners' – and the genocidal truth of the soldier seeking murderous revenge, but also the pressman Merrick dutifully writing down Crook's words and later double-checking with him that they are accurate. Like many revisionist Westerns, the bits it wants to revise are what it deems to be 'sanitised' in this way: typically, unsavoury, unpleasant and brutal aspects of life that cannot be coherently accommodated by positive myths. So *Deadwood*'s version of Wild Bill Hickok is as a depressive compulsive gambler and end-stage alcoholic, Calamity Jane a foul-mouthed, incontinent alcoholic, Seth Bullock an impulsive maniac with little control over his violent temper; most of all, throughout the series we see the constant brutalisation and murder of prostitutes, including the starving to death and public burning of Chinese women. It would be a mistake, however, to claim that *Deadwood*'s primary concern with history is in showing us 'how it really was' since this ambition is in itself in the service of a much larger and more complex meditation on the relationship between the past and the present. The word David Milch used to describe his interest in the Western setting is 'genesis', and the history, geology and historical characters allow him to situate us in a region that is steeped in the idea of origins and new beginnings. This is how (the show seems to say) human beings in a lawless, wild and dangerous environment have to improvise ways of working together and in so doing discover and cultivate structures of adult solidarity and social organisation. This is anchored to a generically ripe historical setting as the stage for the fictional exploration of human nature itself.

31

The issue which emerges then is *why* Milch and the premium cable network Home Box Office (HBO) which funded it created such a show in the early years of the twenty-first century? A full answer would require a more complete sense of how corporate structures get caught up in matters of wider artistic and cultural significance; say, in how they aspire to be beacons, signifiers or translators of the cultural moment. 'What's in it for the company?' is the more prosaic way to put it. This was the issue raised in the press when pre-production of *Deadwood* was announced in 2002. HBO had grown from a subscription channel established in the early 1970s, offering movies and sports events, to a company whose output convinced some scholars to claim that television 'is one of America's most important and provocative art forms'.[19] The shows that made this view plausible were all long-form dramas with strong authorial presence: *The Sopranos* (1999–2007, David Chase), *Six Feet Under* (2001–5, Alan Ball), *The Wire* (2002–8, David Simon) to name the three that represented the first tranche at this pitch of quality. These and other HBO dramas and comedy shows were emphatically 'adult', meaning that they were explicit in their depiction of sex, obscenity and violence. However, by 2002, there were concerns about the renewal of its dramatic stable and the announcement of a Western created by Milch whose previous success was in the cop-show genre, notably *NYPD Blue* (1993–2005), seemed to be an anomaly amid this crop of contemporary adult drama: was this to be '*Sopranos* Go West' or '*Six Feet Under* Boot Hill'?[20] In this context, it is surprising that when the pilot was first aired in March 2003 (debuting at 10.00 pm Sunday night directly after *The Sopranos*), it came under such heavy scrutiny for its depiction of sex, violence and most of all its language. It was not the intensity of the obscenity that caused *Deadwood* so much trouble but the issue of its historical *credibility*: did they really talk (swear) like that? For example, Robert Blanco argues in a preview piece:

> Anyone who thinks that the language in [*NYPD*] *Blue* is blue will be surprised to see how much farther Milch can go when he's freed from broadcast TV's euphemisms – both in terms of the frequency of the profanities and their rap-video modernity. Indeed the shocking thing about *Deadwood* is that even with *The Sopranos* as a lead in, the show's language is still shocking. Perhaps this is the way people really spoke in 1876 Deadwood, but TV isn't a research paper, and shows don't run with footnotes and annotations. Many viewers are likely to feel that Milch has failed to make the expletive-laden dialogue play as believable. Equally many are likely to find it off-putting, whether they believe it or not. It's just one more barrier for a genre that already has a problem connecting with a modern audience.[21]

Milch fronted a press preview screening insisting 'that was the way they spoke' and was interviewed by Terry Gross on NPR and Tavis Smiley on

PBS, both of whom began by questioning him about the authenticity of the language.[22] After describing HBO as 'very decisive and supportive', Milch's response to Smiley's question about the show's profanity articulates the tension between the desire to be dramatically engaging and the grounding of its reality in historical truth:

> The language is rough … language is precious when you're trying to tell a story, particularly when you're trying to create a reality for the viewer about a world which is different from the viewer's own experience. That's the way they talked. They were outcast. An outcast group tends to develop its own language … . It seemed to me because we associate a particular kind of sanitised language with the Western and this was not going to be a Western like other Westerns it was important to get the language right.[23]

Publicity surrounding *Deadwood*'s first season, including the behind-the-scenes features on the DVD version emphasised the extent of Milch's historical research: over two years researching the history, visiting archives, reading contemporary newspapers, accounts, memoirs, biographies, living in the town. Blanco's sneering reference to 'footnotes and annotations' may refer to a research paper that Milch prepared in late 2003 presumably to counter objections that the language was not credible. It is called 'Profanity in Deadwood' and consists of just over 2,000 words, including bibliography, of closely argued prose that is effectively a creative manifesto for the show itself.

In it, Milch begins by setting the context for the mythic invention of the genre:

> In the latter part of the nineteenth century, accelerated geographical expansion, urbanisation, industrialisation, waves of immigration from Europe and Asia and a revolution in communication all jostled to call into question what America was. Among the 'makers' of American culture, one response was a drive toward organising the American experience into a group of charged metaphors, a simplified idealised, imaginative orthodoxy for the public to embrace and consume.

33

This mythologised version of the West was articulated in Wild West
shows, dime-store novels and eventually film and television. According
to Donald Sassoon, it became 'a genre which demands prolific
production' and its longevity and generativity as a cultural form is
exemplified by Owen Wister's 1902 novel, *The Virginian*, which was
translated across the world, adapted as a successful play, five films and a
television series. Despite its grounding in North American experiences
and locations, the genre was immediately successful as an international
form (for example the novels of Karl May in Germany) and continues to
be so. The genre's success is no doubt in part because it repeatedly stages
in a variety of narrative designs the foundational confrontation between
nature and civilisation, exemplified by James Fenimore Cooper's Natty
Bumpo. According to Robert Pippin:

> Mythic accounts are about events in the remote past of decisive
> significance for the present (often about foundings) and they assume that
> the course of these events is the result of actions undertaken by heroes of
> superhuman abilities. The tone is one of elevated seriousness, so the form
> of such storytelling is usually epic.[24]

This is certainly true of the great movie Westerns – *Red River* (1947), *The
Man Who Shot Liberty Valance* (1962), *The Searchers* (1956) – that
Pippin demonstrates offer sustained and complex modes of thinking
about our participation in and allegiance to social political life.
In 'Profanity in Deadwood', this mythologised version reached an
'apotheosis' in Hollywood movies and television between 1940 and
1970. Although such productions wore 'the trappings of history', their
connection to lived experience was minimal. Even more estrangement
from that experience happened because the Production Code which
governed the industry for most of this period further sanitised this
mythologised image of the West; Milch quotes from the Code's rules on
Obscenity ('Obscenity in fact, that is, in spoken word, gesture, episode,
plot is against divine and human law, and hence altogether outside the
range of subject matter or treatment') and contrasts this with the vast

evidence, documented by H. L. Mencken, Daniel Boorstin and accounts in the Library of Congress American Memory projects that profanity was a constant and pervasive dimension of pioneer life, particularly in mining camps.[25] For Milch, these sources prove beyond doubt that 'profanity … was of the essence of the westering experience'. He quotes one account of the Californian Rush by the reformer Eliza Burhans Farnham:

> The first years of the gold emigration … . Scheming, gaming, profanity, licentiousness, and intemperance, reared themselves to such frightful stature that one could not easily see how they were to be laid low again … . Then the profanity, one heard on every hand, was shocking. It seemed really wonderful how many oaths could be crowded into the commonest conversation without excluding the words that expressed ideas.

Milch argues that Deadwood was filled with outcasts, criminals and rebels drawn to the gold strike in a camp outside the law, and that profanity, slang and jargon were forms of maintaining isolation and separateness from the world which they had quit or which had rejected them. As with Ellsworth's 'hammered shit' declaration, profanity was a kind of armour which enabled conversation without revealing identity.

35

All of this seems credible, but the issue was not so much *did* the miners swear a lot, which was uncontroversial, but did they swear *in this way*. Milch's response is to point out that, given that the words certainly existed then and would have been known to Deadwood's inhabitants then it makes sense, given the historical context he has outlined that they would have used them. The essay concludes:

> If, as seems demonstrable, words like *prick, cunt, shit, fuck,* and *cocksucker* would have been in common usage in the time and place in which *Deadwood* is set, then, like any words, in form and frequency their expression will be governed by the personality of a given character, imagined by the author with whatever imperfection, as the character is shaped and tested in the crucible of experience. The goal is not to offend but to realise the character's full humanness.

Of course *nobody talks like that*: not the way they do in *Deadwood* or in *Measure for Measure* or *Billy Budd, Sailor*. But then realism is not primarily about documentary accuracy, but is rather a means to the truth, an attempt to shape and pattern the congealed forms of historical human life in ways that cast light upon them.

In this respect, the most interesting part of the document is a paragraph on the third page seemingly separate from the main argument and evidence, which is an outright defence of realism as an artistic principle. Here, Milch argues that 'the cascading pluralisms', which prompted the mythologising of the West, also stimulated another response from artists who 'sought an organizing principle for their art in objectively portraying life as it was lived', and quotes William Dean Howells's notion of storytelling as 'nothing more than the truthful treatment of material'. While acknowledging that realism is only one way to tell a story, Milch asserts that 'it has a respectable history' and lists those writers 'operating in the realistic mode … [who] have explored subjects from frontier life to the nuanced consciousness of international aesthetes to the struggles of the urban underclass'. The names he lists are emblems of a tradition in which Milch sees himself writing: Mark Twain, Henry James, Stephen Crane, Frank Norris, Theodore Dreiser, Jack London and Hamlin Garland. 'If', writes Milch, 'characters like those portrayed in *Deadwood* did use profanity and obscenity, then the storyteller who aspires to realism will show them doing so'. I take from this that Milch is claiming membership among the tradition he cites (in other conversations on the topic he would add more contemporary writers such as Jimmy Breslin and Hubert Selby), but it is one earned more in the pursuit of objective portrayal and dedication to the truth of the characters than it is to the reality of the past. The tension is formed in giving artistic shape to the factual past and in so doing, changing it, so that it 'takes wing', a life of its own. The profanity makes this issue stark and immediate for any viewer, since the language we hear sings with the eloquence of its artistic shaping more than its sense of historical verity. On the one hand, Milch wants to avoid the sanitised, mythologised, industrially compromised version of the

West that he claims has hitherto dominated; but on the other, he does
not want to relinquish the artistic autonomy that allows creative work
to organise and give form to the mostly chaotic immediacy of the
historical truth of the world.

Strange as it may seem, this approach has an affinity with the
thinking of Hungarian Marxist, György Lukács, who follows German
idealist philosopher Hegel, in thinking that mythic narratives rely on
issues of universal significance (such as the founding of a community)
being dependent on the actions of individuals. According to Pippin
in Hegel's historical time 'the past is more like geological layers that
accumulate and still make their presence felt, still exert a kind of
pressure on action and have some hold on our imagination'.[26] Lukács
takes this sense of history in order to focus on

> the analysis of the authentic work of art as a special type of ideal-cultural
> objectivisation characterised by the organic unity of its form and content
> allowing a truth of universal significance to appear in a directly
> apprehensible, sensuous-concrete embodiment.[27]

37

Central to this is the aesthetic process of mimesis, the shaping of reality
and its relating back to the human subject: Milch's 'full humanness'.
In attempting to dramatise the pressure of those geological layers, as
well as aspiring to a unity of form and content, Milch was going beyond
a revisionist Western that counterposed chaos to harmony (as some
critics have read it). To make sense of this aspiration it is necessary to
consider Milch's background in the world of American literary and
television fiction.

David Milch

A full appreciation of Milch's contribution to the development of
television art requires a book-long study; all I can do here is sketch some
of his career signposts relevant to an understanding of *Deadwood*. At

the time of the return of the show for its second season he was the subject of several features, profiles, interviews and commentaries, which variously detailed his colourful background.[28] Born to a Jewish family in Buffalo, New York State in 1945, he is the son of a clinical professor of surgery who had family connections to the world of organised crime, and was also addicted to various painkilling substances. By his own account, Milch was introduced by his father to the world of gambling at the Saratoga race-course when he was five; shortly after he was sent to summer camp, where he suffered the attentions of the camp counsellor.[29] Unsurprisingly Milch's childhood and teenage behaviour was erratic – he would ingest whatever medication he could find in his father's medicine cabinet, he was arrested by police for underage drinking, and he would be caught trying to slip over the Canadian border to get to a racetrack.

Academically, Milch was outstanding. He studied English at Yale, graduating top in his year and winning the senior prize. It was here that he experienced the teaching of Robert Penn Warren, Southern Poet, one of the founders of the New Criticism approach to literary analysis, the only person to win Pulitzer Prizes for both fiction and poetry, and who was to remain his friend and artistic touchstone for the rest of his life. Milch had already begun to write as an undergraduate, working on a novel, *The Groundlings*, the first two chapters of which formed the dissertation for his Master of Fine Arts degree in Creative Writing at the prestigious Iowa Writers' Workshop, where he went on to work as a teaching fellow. By all accounts, he was a dazzling student and teacher, although some claim his teachers and colleagues at Iowa, including Richard Yates and Kurt Vonnegut, resented his Ivy League pedigree.[30] Academic prowess did not mute his appetites for alcohol, drugs and gambling, which were to occupy his life for the next three decades. He evidently found stability back at Yale in the late 1960s and 70s, working as research assistant for Warren, Cleanth Brooks and R. W. B Lewis on various scholarly books. Warren and Brooks were the leading lights of New Criticism, which, although beginning to wane in the face of emerging Freudian and structuralist approaches to 'the text', was still the dominant form of literary analysis at the time. It was an approach that stressed the close observation and analysis of poetry and literary texts, counterposing their unity and harmony to the dislocating nature of modern life. Working with Warren, Milch found 'the gift of thinking the best of people and somehow that made you be your best, or at least want to be'.[31] As mentioned, he was research assistant on Warren, Brooks and Lewis's monumental four-volume survey, *American Literature: The Makers and the Making* where he received another, deeper education in the shape and nature of the American literary tradition.[32] He was also a vital assistant to Lewis in the writing of his Pulitzer Prize-winning biography of Edith Wharton.[33] With Lewis, he pitched the idea of a ten-part television miniseries on the lives of the James family (Henry, William and Alice) to the National Endowment for the Arts, to be produced by Merchant–Ivory.[34] It was around this time that Milch's father committed suicide.[35]

Such a background, steeped in the tradition of American letters, would seem to point to a career as a novelist; but it was not until 1982, when he was well into his thirties, that he began to write for network television on Steven Bochco's pioneering series, *Hill Street Blues* (NBC, 1981–7). A writer's strike made this opening possible when Jeffrey Lewis, a former Yale roommate and producer on the show, called him up to ask him to write a script. Despite his lack of experience in the trade, Milch's first script, for the episode 'Trial by Fury', won the 1982 Emmy Award for Best Dramatic Episode as well as the Humanitas Prize. This immediate success secured Milch's career in the industry in which he has been tremendously productive ever since. In the 1990s, Milch partnered again with Bochco in the development and production of *NYPD Blue* which was ground-breaking for a network show, in its depiction of adult topics – once again, violence, nudity and bad language – and revived the fortunes of long-form television drama at a point when it had seemed to be in decline. *NYPD Blue*'s central character, the alcoholic and racist Andy Sipowicz, remains one of the epic creations of television drama – epic in that intimate sense of taking the smaller, less heroic-seeming characters and discovering in their flaws and existential crises an entire

David Milch, Robert Penn Warren, Dennis Franz as Andy Sipowicz in *NYPD Blue*

universe of grievance, despair, hurt, as well as aspiration to self-improvement, equanimity, even joy. As played by Dennis Franz, Sipowicz is an Everyman whose defects of the spirit earned the show its reputation for the eloquent depiction of masculinity and authority in decline. Sipowicz has a charm in his sometimes repugnant 'obstinate finality' as a human, a trait that we can see develop in a way less camouflaged by modernity in the character of Al Swearengen.

After leaving *NYPD Blue* in 1998 (although the show continued for five more seasons), Milch signed a multiyear contract with

Paramount to develop television series, resulting in *Big Apple* (CBS, 2001). This had a contemporary New York setting which formed the backdrop for what was on the surface a drama about the FBI and NYPD working together in order to combat organised crime; but as the poster for the show – which depicts Adam and Eve in front of the New York city skyline – hints, its deeper interest is in the exchange and ownership of knowledge itself. Here Milch, now free from substance addiction, became bolder in articulating his thematic ambitions and although *Big Apple* was cancelled, it was clear he was extending his artistic wings.[36]

The attacks of 9/11 inflected Milch's creative orientation in a significant way; he claimed it was now impossible to connect to an audience through contemporary drama since, 'in the aftermath of 9/11, people are so guarded emotionally, savaged by what they experienced through TV [coverage of the attacks on the World Trade Center]'. In this view, contemporary dramatic settings simply could not live up to the unfolding drama of that kind of news. Teaching again at screenwriting workshops and at universities in America and Europe, the newly sober Milch would use his charismatic oratory to promote writing techniques for new and emerging writers, as well as training a regularly renewed clutch of writing interns at his Los Angeles production company, Red Board. Reading transcripts of some of these events, it is clear that by the turn of the century, Milch had developed a coherent and commanding authority over his belief in the provenance and power of his art.

At the same time, in the television industry, Milch pitched his next project to the cable network HBO which, as noted above, had developed a reputation as a hospitable stable for television auteurs or 'show runners' (those who direct the ultimate artistic trajectory of a collaborative writing and production process). The project was another cop show, one set in the very distant past; the log line was 'St Paul Gets Busted', and the setting concerned city cops – the *cohorts urbanae* – at the time of Nero's Rome. In interviews, in which he makes light of the strangeness of *Deadwood*'s origins, Milch claims Chris Albrecht and Carolyn Strauss, the senior executives at HBO, listened politely to the pitch before informing him that they had already commissioned a show

41

with that setting, a co-production with the BBC called *Rome* (BBC/HBO, 2005–7).[37] 'I was interested in how those who were assigned to enforce order proceeded in the absence of any law at all …', claims Milch and so, when it was suggested that he might develop the same themes in a different setting, he eventually decided on doing a Western: 'this seemed like an analogous situation, because Deadwood was a community that explicitly renounced law'.[38] Almost by accident then, Milch began research on what was to be a founding narrative in a genre explicitly concerned with America's origins. Although he later claimed not to like the Western genre, Milch recruited legendary producer of film and television Westerns at Paramount, A. C. Lyles, as a consultant on the show.

This outline of the shape of Milch's career and his achievements allows us to consider his 'Profanity in Deadwood' in its proper context. The document is a complex gesture in itself – it is not addressed to anyone but it bears the weight of a response to a demand. Milch was not simply, as some accounts have it, a Yale English Literature academic wanting to shock the bourgeois audience with obscenity – he was a highly esteemed veteran of the television industry. In its detailing of the industrial pressures which compromised the truth-telling abilities of the Western genre, it also constitutes a warning, however obscure, to the contemporary manifestation of that industry not to mess with artistic ambition: it claims that there is another tradition, that of imaginative storytelling that demands prior fealty. While it is tempting to follow theatre impresario Jack Langrishe's assessment of the town as 'yearning for elevation and festering with wealth' and apply it to television, it was also an industry which was beginning to produce significant artistic cultural forms, reaching beyond its earlier admirable but lesser achievements.

It is not my intention, because of Milch's earlier role in tending the literary canon of America at Yale, to conflate literary values with those appropriate to an assessment of a television show. But the two need not be mutually exclusive. Long-form television drama thrives on character development, and the arc of character can take shape over many episodes and seasons. As television scholars have acknowledged, this places serial television drama, like the serialised novels of Eliot, Dostoevsky, Dickens and Melville in a special relationship to history.[39] Their ability to encompass the broad slices of time, to articulate the sweep of history and weave complex patterns of repetition and development that build and then draw on our memories of their fictional action is central to their unique commitment to storytelling which is both intimate in its reliance on the repeated thickening of character interiority, and epic in its location of universal themes tied to individual action. It is not a distortion or betrayal of the show's origins in the medium of television to locate *Deadwood*'s achievement among that of great literature, nor is this necessarily saying that the only way television can be regarded as valuable is when it mimics the language, themes and forms of the printed word. This does not exclude it from admission to the canon as a *television* classic because that is the medium in which it also finds artistic roots and patterns. This show rejects the hygienic purity of medium specificity in favour of a mode of storytelling privileging the spectacle of words and language that are critically tied to matters of power, to identity and to settlement. It is a spectacle staged by charismatic individuals vying for their place in the world of words.

43

3 Al and Seth

Early in the pilot episode, we see Calamity Jane ask a family on a wagon if there is a shortcut into camp; they tell her they are leaving it, as if to say this is no place for a family (or family viewing). 'We go back to Minnesota', says the matriarch in a heavy accent (we later discover they are 'squareheads' – Norwegians); this is the Metz family who are massacred and dismembered on the Spearfish road.[40] Ma and Pa and three blonde children, the Metzes are the only conventional family we ever glimpse in the show and they are brutally erased from the world apart from their youngest, a little girl called Sofia (Bree Seanna Wall). Nonetheless *Deadwood* is a kind of family story, one where the 'family values' of love, loyalty, jealousy, betrayal and grief are developed through the growing interactions and intersections of its main characters. One way to characterise the show is as a gradual coming together of a community whose bonds of loyalty and trust are forged through sharing an often violent history, rather than established by the authority of pre-existing blood ties. So *Deadwood* begins with a family literally torn apart and then proceeds to make one anew; the formation of the Deadwood family begins with the dismemberment of the Metz one.

We first hear of the massacre when Bullock, Star and Reverend Smith encounter an unkempt rider in the street who reports, 'I seen a terrible thing tonight … white people dead and scalped … man, woman and children with their arms and legs hacked off.' The man repeats his story in Nuttall's *No. 10 Saloon* where Hickok is losing at poker to Jack McCall (Garret Dillahunt), the man who will eventually murder him.

Suspicious of the validity of the story, Bullock and Hickok lead a posse to
ride out with the man to the site of the killing. Meanwhile – and here
Deadwood displays the ease with which it will cross-weave and intersect
its strands of plot through the circulation of knowledge – one of
Swearengen's minions, Johnny Burns, brings him the dope addict Jimmy
Irons (Dean Rader-Duval), who has witnessed the hand talking about the
massacre in the bar. Swearengen is not, however, fazed by news of the
massacre – instead he is enraged by Burns's slackness in failing to contain
that knowledge since he's allowed Irons to blab the news downstairs:

> SWEARENGEN: *[punches Burns in the face]* You let him tell a few people
> downstairs *before* you bring this to me? … How many people you think the
> people he talked to have talked to by now? I guarantee at this minute my
> entire fucking action downstairs is fucked up. Nobody's drinking, nobody's
> gambling, and nobody's chasing tail. *I have to deal with that.*   ('Deadwood')

In his commentary on this scene, David Milch remarks,

45

> That's the way a dysfunctional family works. There's always one kid in the
> family that gets the shit kicked out of him. That's his job. Now the other kid
> in the family explains Dad to the kid who's always getting hit

– this last point as Dority says to Burns, 'He's got a lot on his mind
Johnny.' (In the script, Burns nurses his injury and 'his lower lip
protrudes and trembles like a boy after his Pa's given him a licking'.)
Swearengen is without doubt the patriarch of the camp, a moody Dad,
whose shifting temperament requires studied respect or else violent
verbal rebuke or worse is in prospect. His central concern is with what
he calls in these early episodes his 'operation', an economy dependent
above all on the ever-changing climate of mood and feeling that the
miners bring and which stimulates them to gamble, whore and drink.
Maintaining and expanding the success of the saloon and its tendrils of
influence and nourishment in the supply of drugs, prostitution and
booze requires an intimate knowledge of the depth and nature of base

human appetites in order to efficiently exploit them. In order to undo
the damage of the news of the massacre, Swearengen goes downstairs
and addresses the patrons in his bar in terms that amplify the danger of
riding out with Hickok's posse and incentivise the pleasures in staying,
and spending, at the *Gem*:

> SWEARFNGEN: I know word's circulating Indians killed a family on the
> Spearfish road. Now it's not for me to tell anyone in this camp what to do,
> as much as I don't want people getting their throats cut, scalps lifted, or
> any other godless thing that these godless bloodthirsty heathens do, or
> if someone wants to ride out in darkest night. But I will tell you this.
> *I* would use tonight to get myself organised and ride out in the morning
> clearheaded. And starting tomorrow morning, I will offer a personal fifty
> dollar bounty for every decapitated head of as many of these godless
> heathen cocksuckers as anyone can bring in tomorrow, with no upper limit.
> And that's all I say on that subject, except the next round is on The House,
> and God rest the souls of that family. And pussy's half price next fifteen
> minutes.   ('Deadwood')

The long-term continuance of his operation to his satisfaction
dominates Al's thinking throughout *Deadwood* and it is fair to say that
most of the spine of the show's storytelling is organised around his
paranoia in response to threats real or imagined to his business. These
machinations are at their most convoluted and deadly in the first season
(whereas in the second and third, his allegiance is to the camp against
outside interests of Yankton and Hearst); in summary, they give an
outline of the complex nature of the show's early plotting:

1. In a set-up land sale, he tricks Brom Garret (Timothy Omundson), a
wealthy tenderfoot from the East, into buying a gold claim after Dority
has 'salted' the land with nuggets. Irishman Tim Driscoll (Dan
Hildebrand) pretends to be the claim's drunken owner, and Swearengen
uses E. B. Farnum (William Sanderson), unctuous owner of the *Grand
Central Hotel* (and his source of news about new arrivals in the camp),

as a rival bidder in order to get Garret to buy the claim at an inflated price. After Driscoll improvises during the con and asks for a larger cut, Swearengen orders Dority to murder him; Farnum lets the latter into Driscoll's hotel room, where he is knifed to death. After some perfunctory efforts to prospect, Garret, realising he has been duped into buying a worthless claim, tries to enlist the help of Hickok; when he has no luck hiring the gunfighter he threatens Swearengen with his mortal enemies the Pinkertons.[41] In response, Swearengen has Dority murder him while they reconnoitre the cliffs around his claim; but after he kills him Dority discovers there are in fact huge quantities of gold there. This is unknown to his widow, Alma Garret, who enlists Hickok to ascertain the claim's true value. This plot, which plays out over the first seven episodes intersects with –

2. The Metz family are massacred outside of the camp by road agents who work for Swearengen but who have not cleared this operation in advance with him. When Hickok and Bullock ride out with the posse to the kill site they discover a survivor, the young girl who locked eyes with Jane as the family fled the camp. Although she is a squarehead, Swearengen realises she is a carrier of lethal information and could reveal that white bandits were to blame, destabilising the camp and disrupting his business; as he tells the leader of the bandits, Persimmon Phil (Joe Chrest):

> I don't want that kid telling people in English or squarehead or drawing fuckin' pictures in the shit with twigs about how it wasn't Indians that killed her people but whites. *[He punches Phil in the ear, knocks him off his chair and grabs him by the collar.]* This camp could be up for grabs, God knows what those cocksuckers are up to, Hickok and the rest and what I'm going to have to do about it. And just when I need to keep my head clear you give me these bags of shit to hold! ('Deep Water')

He then tells Dority to kill the child, who is being cared for by Doc Cochran and Jane, although after they spirit her out of the camp,

Swearengen instead decides to kill Phil. In the meantime, acting together, Hickok and Bullock kill the man who originally told them about the massacre in a street gunfight (the only one of its kind in this Western). This plot converges with Plot 1 when Hickok is murdered and Jane leaves the child with Alma Garret, who is a laudanum addict. Swearengen orders his favourite whore Trixie to load her up with dope, thus making her vulnerable to Farnum's attempts, as Al's secret proxy, to buy the now fabulously rich claim back. But Trixie instead defies him, helping Alma to kick the dope, and it is Bullock, on the recommendation of Hickok, who takes over the task of assaying the claim.

By the eighth episode, both plotlines have done a good job of bringing various characters in the camp into much closer relationships. What the script describes as 'the labyrinthine resourcefulness of Swearengen's paranoia' about the threats to his operation remains at the centre of them all: from the 'dirt worshipping heathens', from competition to his operation in the opening of Cy Tolliver's upmarket *Bella Union* saloon, from corrupt political forces attempting to annex the camp, from the Pinkertons, to questions about the loyalty and efficiency of his staff. In the first episodes, it is Swearengen's fear of the potential power of Hickok and Bullock as guns for hire working together that causes him great anxiety, hence the early series of confrontations he has with Star and Bullock as they try to buy the lot they are renting from him. As a pure capitalist, Swearengen grasps the shifting valency of human desires, whose meaning and origins are often obscure to those who possess them: this is the psychological métier of the skilled retailer, amplified into epic form. Naturally this gift tends toward paranoia. Early versions of the script describe how the 'still encroaching fear' and 'haunted' nature of Swearengen and his vigilance against those who would disrupt or disturb his world operate at the micro levels of syntax and semantics. This is evident in the scene where Bullock and Star try to make an offer on the lot to Swearengen as he pours them drinks in his bar:

SWEARENGEN: I guess before I made a price I'd want to know if you boys had unnamed partners.

BULLOCK: Why?
SWEARENGEN: I think specifically Wild Bill Hickok. Didn't you and
Bullock act together in the street this morning?
STAR: No we just *met* Wild Bill Hickok.
BULLOCK: *[To Star]* What business of *that* is *his*?
SWEARENGEN: You mean, what business of *mine* is *that*.
BULLOCK: *[furious]* Don't tell me what *the fuck* I mean.
SWEARENGEN: Not a tone to get a deal done.   ('Deep Water')

Swearengen is vulnerable to paranoia because of the thing that makes
him such a successful saloon keeper; he is an athlete of perception.
Many of the emblematic shots of Swearengen involve him watching or
seeing, not least the iconic shots of him surveying the camp like an
emperor from his vantage point on the balcony at the *Gem*.

This quality of acute, devilish perspicacity, an aliveness
to the words, sights, smells and sounds of his environment is most
evident in what we might call the 'Al's Office' scenes. It is here,
usually seated at a desk littered with books and papers, that he
conducts his most serious business and those in attendance are subject
to intense scrutiny. The first such scene, with the doomed Tim Driscoll

49

Al's office

establishes a pattern, which is developed and elaborated over the rest
of the series; the victim sits opposite Al whose gaze so thoroughly
unnerves its object that they wither and abandon dissembling beneath
it. Driscoll acquits himself so badly that Swearengen has Dority kill
him that night. Such interviews act as a means of sounding out the
origin, extent and resilience of the interlocutor's deceit; sometimes Al
can literally smell the lies. In 'Mister Wu' (1–10) Jimmy Irons, who has
stolen a consignment of drugs en route to Swearengen, tries feebly to
resist this perceptual spotlight:

> SWEARENGEN: You've been wrong since you walked in here, you know that
> Jimmy, don't you?
> IRONS: What do you mean Mr Swearengen?
> SWEARENGEN: You've been lying. This room stinks right now of cat-piss so
> bad I want to burn the fucking building down.
> IRONS: I'm nervous sir, I'm always nervous around you.
> SWEARENGEN: Nervousness don't cause that smell. *Lying* causes a cat-
> piss smell.   ('Mister Wu')

So disrupted is Irons by Swearengen's power that he soils himself
and is forced to jump off the balcony. His office is also the setting for
discoursing in front of his minions. In an early scene when Swearengen
is trying to figure out who betrayed him by selling the hotel next to his
joint to Cy Tolliver, we see him leap on the redundancy of repeated
exposition (a familiar technique in film and television):

> SWEARENGEN: I want to know who did that legwork.
> FARNUM: You hit the nail square, Al. Whoever went between them *Bella
> Union* people and Artie Simpson would be a prime source of information.
> SWEARENGEN: Do not repeat back to me what *I* just said in different
> fucking words!   ('Reconnoitring the Rim')

Such scenes occur throughout the show, culminating in one late in the
final season, in which Swearengen is confronted by no less than Wyatt

Earp (Gale Harold) across his desk, and effortlessly pierces the thin fabric of his lies, delivering the *coup de grâce* to the past, present and future of his mendacity with the gravelly realism of a wise king: 'I'll test the sense of it that knows more of this place, and I guess every other, than you do', while playing with a fly swat; it has become that easy for him. Of course, such two-hander interview scenes are a classic television form and their effectiveness as drama depends crucially on the ability of the actors to carry and rise to the close attention of the camera.

Ian McShane's performance is one of the finest and most memorable in screen history; it is an extraordinary achievement in realising the complexity of Milch's words with consistently credible and convincing skill and with a voice that holds in tension a quality of rich menace and intimate charm. It transforms what we think we know about villainy and heroism so that by the final episodes we may even come to accept the extraordinary claim, as Milch puts it, that Swearengen was capable of becoming President. As is true with so many other aspects of *Deadwood*, the comparisons with the emblems of high art can be sustained here: McShane's Swearengen embodies the compelling charisma of articulate villainy worthy of Milton's Satan.[42] Like that Satan, Swearengen is rhetorically gifted and when he speaks with that rich bass vibrancy which floats from his chest to hum in his mouth, it is irresistible even when we do not immediately grasp its meaning. He is physically lethal as well; in the first season, we see him murder three people directly (Persimmon Phil, Jimmy Irons and Reverend Smith), while several more die on his orders, as well as brutalise Trixie, and regularly punch his underlings. He is an elementally ferocious, self-sustaining capitalist and never as evil as when we see him push past Jane to get at the injured Norwegian child to – do what? What is terrifying is that at that moment, like Jane we are paralysed, completely uncertain as to whether or not he will slaughter the child in front of our eyes. Here and elsewhere, we get a sense of his unencumbered power, able to journey where it wishes and alight on whatever victims serve its interest. In an office scene which is shot to underline his potency, Swearengen intimidates the oleaginous innkeeper

51

E. B. Farnum (his most frequent interlocutor in these early episodes) reminding him of his omnipotence:

> FARNUM: You tell me Al, have you a doubt or misgiving?
> SWEARENGEN: Generally if I have a misgiving or a doubt I kill the cocksucker I have a doubt and misgiving about.
> FARNUM: But these are special circumstances.
> SWEARENGEN: I don't know what you mean by special circumstances. If I want to I can burn the whole fucking camp down.
> FARNUM: Yes you can.
> SWEARENGEN: Cut *your* throat first and then burn down the whole fucking camp.　　　　　('Reconnoitring the Rim')

As he speaks, Swearengen manoeuvres behind the shaking Farnum, even loosing his tongue from his mouth with serpentine deliberation to whisper up close in his left ear. McShane uses the repetitions in the words he is given not only to amplify menace but to insist on the implacable certainty of Swearengen's thoughts – so that what might be mere threats, don't at all *sound* like that; the second time he says 'the … whole … fucking … camp', it is delivered piece by piece as if he is lighting fires, one by one.

The casting was fortuitous in a number of ways. Milch originally wanted an American actor – the real Swearengen was from Iowa – and chose Ed O'Neill (of *Married with Children*, 1987–97 and also the star of *Big Apple*): certainly O'Neill's stature and capacity for menace and charm would have worked well (as indeed it did when he played the role of retired cop Bill Jacks in Milch's *John from Cincinnati*, 2007); when this was not viable, his second choice was Powers Boothe, who was unavailable for the pilot but who instead later joined the cast as Swearengen's rival Cy Tolliver (allowing the development of an alternative register of evil). McShane's pedigree was perfect despite being an Englishman: born in Lancashire, the son of a Manchester United winger (and clearly inheriting that athleticism), his early acting tended to roles which emphasised a handsome intelligence that was

52

always freighted with a dark magnetic charm: he played, for example, Heathcliff in the BBC's 1967 adaptation of *Wuthering Heights*, a politically articulate Judas Iscariot in the miniseries *Jesus of Nazareth* (1977), and most famously in British television brought to life Jonathan Gash's picaresque antique dealer and loveable rogue *Lovejoy* (1986–94). As I have noted elsewhere this casting also points to a literary heritage; there is, in his swarthy intelligence a gesture to *Oliver Twist*'s brutal Bill Sikes fused with the intelligent organisational capacity of Fagin.[43] This heritage is acknowledged physically in casting McShane: compare him to Robert Newton's Sikes in *Oliver Twist* (David Lean, 1948) or better still, Oliver Reed's version of that character in *Oliver!* (Carol Reed, 1968). But McShane takes this further by relishing the full corporeal reality of Swearengen, letting his fat, hairy belly literally hang out, and showing his unembarrassed delight in the regular morning piss into his pot which reinforces the regressive animality of territory being marked, his stream itself a vulgar measure of continuing vitality.

These performances and characters are of course to some extent bound by the forms in which they appear: in novels, plays and films, characters and the actors playing them tend to know their complete story, their destination, where they are 'coming in to land'. This permits the actor to telescope and plant (or have to conceal) aspects of the character's destiny within a performance, but it also concentrates and constrains a character, shutting their possibilities down. Equally, the risk in basing one's drama on real people is that those destinations (and deviations therefrom) can begin to intrude on the natural unfolding of the drama, and over-inform the actor's view of the character. By contrast, long-form serial drama is rarely written with an ultimate destination finalised, unusually for fiction, it often comes to the consumer with its characters and plots unfinished. Thankfully Swearengen (the real one was found penniless and murdered several years after the time *Deadwood* is set) in Milch and McShane's hands never feels 'finished' in this way; there is always more to him that becomes available.

53

Hickok by contrast, is a fixed entity, his destination clear and
well known: shot dead over a poker game at Nuttall's *No. 10 Saloon* by
the coward Jack McCall on 2 August 1876. In many ways Hickok is
offered to us in the standard revisionist garb that deflates the myth by
emphasising personal flaws such as his alcoholism and gambling as
well as the nasty obscenity of his language. We see this when he insults
McCall (who has minor facial deformities) after finally beating him
at poker:

> MCCALL: Well, that's one in a row for you Wild Bill. Who's hungry? – what
> the hell damn time is it anyways?
> HICKOK: Sure you want to quit playing Jack? Game's all that's between you
> and gettin' called a cunt. That dropped eye of yours looks like the hood of a
> cunt to me, Jack. When you talk your mouth is like a cunt moving.
> MCCALL: I ain't gonna get in no gunfight with you Hickok.
> HICKOK: But you will run your cunt mouth at me. And I will take it play
> poker.   ('Reconnoitring the Rim')

54

In the above scene, the script describes Hickok's voice as 'heavy
with sleeplessness and alcoholism past alleviation by drink'. Keith
Carradine's performance is masterful in this respect, emphasising
someone stuck in time, his tall body maintaining a still, steady fixity as if
he were a waxwork figure or a museum exhibit already past death and
hung in a display case.

McCall by contrast, has the fast but dopey motion of an
irritant creature, say a tic or a housefly; filthy and rootless, he represents
the danger of being a free-floating soul, unbound to a code, group or
aspiration beyond his own instinctual desire to irritate and inflame.
While McCall in his filthy mediocrity is clearly *of* the camp in ways
Hickok is not, they both share a rootlessness, an unfitness for the
mercantile environment, where one has to partake of the ordinary,
mostly dull, repetitious effort of work. McCall appears to have no
occupation outside of poker. Hickok's co-dependent companion, the
grizzled Charlie Utter tries to monetise his celebrity, but the gunfighter

Often isolated in the shot, Hickok is the last of his kind

resists this 'shilling for the house'. His preferred role is the elegiac, laconic enforcer, where one simple line carries a concentrated form of authority: 'I'll guarantee your scalp', he says to the road agent before leading the posse that rescues the little Metz girl; he then executes the man in the street in the only scene in the show reminiscent of the classic Western gunfight. A point is made by cutting between this very public killing on the side of Public Right, and shots of Dan Dority skulking back after having stabbed Tim Driscoll to death in his bed on the side of Private Whim. Hickok also kills the agent's brother, who Swearengen sends to assassinate Hickok, saying no more than, 'He meant me harm.' Most portentously, after Alma Garret has hired him to assess Swearengen's intentions in buying back the gold claim, his warning to her to leave town comes in the same tight, enigmatic form:

> HICKOK: You know the sound of thunder, don't you Mrs Garret?
> ALMA: Of course.
> HICKOK: Can you imagine that sound if I ask you to?
> ALMA: Yes I can Mr Hickok.
> HICKOK: Your husband and me had this talk and I told *him* to head home to avoid a dark result. But I didn't say it in thunder. Ma'am. *Listen to the thunder.* ('Here Was a Man')

The elegiac gravitas of the gunfighter who knows death is substituted for the continued life that requires the regular effort of work. Utter realises this when he asks Bullock for his secret: '[you] get along with people, turn a dollar, look out for yourself. He don't know how to do that. See what I'm saying? So, I'd like to know your secret so's then I can tell it to Bill.'

Bullock, then, is a transitional figure; like Hickok he is a cop, a man who can enforce order through his skill with violence, but his entire rationale for moving to Deadwood was to become a shopkeeper, not a lawman. Timothy Olyphant is interesting in this respect since much of his gait, gesture and tone channels those lone enforcers of right in the Western, most emblematically portrayed by Clint Eastwood. This quality is reinforced visually by a repeated shot of Bullock walking with determined purpose through Deadwood, while the rest of the busy camp continues around him – he is, in this striding mode, hostage to his own purposes, drives and interests rather than those of the camp. A silent exterior masks and, in its stillness, implies an unspecified energy and power which dominates the spaces around it and confuses those who interact with him; he is not skilled in deceit,

Bullock's rage propels him through the camp

not good at hiding the emotions he projects so powerfully. He is a
conscience in search of an object.

Here handsomeness functions as something of a blank, its
beauty shining so strongly it hides the maniacal violence inside. Already
in the first sequence, with Clell Watson's execution, we see the tension in
Bullock between his self-righteous desire to follow the path of the Law
and his hatred of the mob ('he's hanging under colour of the law … you
loudmouth cocksucker!'), which represents an external manifestation
of the violent rage he feels internally, hence his loud repudiation of its
demands. Such currents of extreme violence and quick temper mean that
the order he could impose through his skills in law enforcement is
constantly threatened by more private loyalties and feelings of
individuated hurt. When Hickok befriends him by naming him after the
place he was Marshal (' "Montana" ok with you?'), he is reinforcing the
identity which Bullock has chosen to leave behind; nonetheless, he seems
attracted to Hickok as a father figure. What that means in this context
is an elder man one finds worthy of fealty and friendship; more than
respect, it implies a willingness to be educated by them. As the story
develops Bullock will have to learn to substitute Hickok – who can teach
him nothing but elegiac one-liners – for Swearengen, whose strategic

57

and social skills, can benefit both of them. The demand that the world bend to your hygienic moral authority is a recipe for constant irascibility. Bullock has to learn to be less fastidious about enacting the demands of his private sense of rectitude. 'What's your partner so mad about all the time?', Swearengen asks Star; 'He's not mad' is the reply – 'Well he's got a mean way of being happy', quips the saloon-keeper. As we have seen, Swearengen's dexterity in verbal contests has Bullock flustered with what the script describes as 'a compelling antagonism toward Swearengen beyond will, logic, justice or injustice'. Bullock's saving difference from Hickok is his recognition of the practical demands of civil and commercial society; when he leaves another almost-violent meeting with Swearengen, he suddenly announces, 'camp needs a bank' and Star, baffled, asks, 'If you can see all these possibilities why get distracted by that saloon-keeper?'

> BULLOCK: What about what he called you? [Swearengen feigned anti-Semitism as a way of breaking tough]
> STAR: I've been called worse by better.   ('Here Was a Man')

Star is grown up enough to set aside personal insult and hurt in order to pursue his interests; Bullock will have to learn to do this, and it is a tough lesson that he struggles to reconcile even in his final lines in the show. That he is able to do it at all distinguishes him, and Swearengen and most of the other characters in Deadwood, from figures like McCall and Hickok who are vulnerable to the life-sapping qualities of the 'idle hours that test us'.

Swearengen's adaptive advantage over Hickok and Bullock is not only his industry but his willingness to endure doing what he does not want to. In what becomes a typical moment of education, he tells Trixie:

> SWEARENGEN: I don't want to talk to these cocksuckers but you have to. In life you have to do a lot of fuckin' things you don't want to do. Many times that's what the fuck life is, one vile fucking task after another. But don't get aggravated. Then the enemy has you by the short hairs.
>
> ('No Other Sons or Daughters')

Al's competitive desire for dominance makes him a Deadwood settler: as he dresses up in his Prince Albert suit (for once without his grubby long johns beneath) in preparation to meet the upmarket *Bella Union* crew, he tells Trixie as she helps him dress, "Where were they when Dan and me were chopping trees in this gulch?"

> SWEARENGEN: Hands all blistered. Bucktooth fucking beavers rolling around in the creek. Slappin' their tails in the water like we was hired entertainment.
>
> TRIXIE: I'd pay a nickel to see you chopping wood.
>
> SWEARENGEN: Don't think I wasn't blow for blow with Dan, I can play that shit when I have to. But I've been to Chicago too. *[raises his arms to his side]* How do I look?
>
> TRIXIE: Like Christ crucified. ('Reconnoitring the Rim')

When Hickok and Swearengen eventually meet for the first and last time in 'Here Was a Man', it is offered to us as a contest of giants (this is the way Farnum and Merrick, who situate themselves as spectators at a distance, seem to take it as well). What is immediately striking about this is the contrast between a legendary gunfighter, sustained by decades of mythologising, being faced down by a saloon-keeper, a figure with a persistent but minimal presence in the genre; indeed, it is rare for the latter to achieve much in the way of screen time. (There are some exceptions of course: the outstanding *Johnny Guitar* (1954) centres around saloon-keeper Vienna, played by Joan Crawford.) This belies the claim that *Deadwood*'s chief revision of the genre is in its depiction of the gritty realism of sex, violence and language; in fact many revisionist Westerns since 1970 (one needs only to mention the names of their directors. Altman, Penn, Peckinpah, Siegel, Leone and Eastwood) have ploughed that land. Eastwood's iconic revisionist masterpiece *Unforgiven* (1992) features a grubby saloon-keeper and pimp Skinny Dubois (Anthony James), but even here the economic underpinnings that give rise to such figures are visible as a background against which ethical and moral dramas dominate. By making

59

Swearengen so compelling, this dimension of the economic/commercial is brought sharply into view. What is different about *Deadwood* is its fundamental shift of emphasis via the charisma of Swearengen to the mercantile dimension of settlement, exploring the nature of capital not as a disrupting, civilising force – say in the depiction of the corrupt railroad or cattle barons – but as a necessary condition of settlement with all its alienating and violent consequences. The economic underpinnings of the social, its metabolic insinuation into all transactions – romantic, inspirational, political, cultural – is foregrounded. In a world built on the immediacy of such transactions, to be at the centre of the social is crucial; for success, one must be a merchant and calibrator of moods and trends. As Swearengen lies to Hickok at their only meeting, it is in this spirit:

> SWEARENGEN: I've been locked in my room weeping, searching my memories as to where my path might have crossed with yours previous. And as to how I might've given offense that you stay in this camp not fifty feet from my joint and never once walk in.
> HICKOK: No poker.
> SWEARENGEN: Is it that simple? Dan, dismantle the titty corner and set up a poker table. ('Here Was a Man')

Here McShane plays him as alertly convivial even though he perceives Hickok as his greatest threat in the camp. This emphasis on monetary and social transaction is a move away from lone, heroic figures like Hickok toward those like Swearengen who, however individually resourceful, derive their power from their skills of communication, sociability and the ability to manage and wield the fruits of adult solidarity they have formed around them. Hickok's social isolation is also his vulnerability and he is shot in a bar that has no equivalent of Dan Dority or Johnny Burns or even E. B. Farnum to protect its boss or watch his back.

We do briefly see Hickok at work, assisting Star and Bullock in building their impressive hardware store; here he is accosted by an irritating fan who says he witnessed him 'blow one cocksucker's head right off his neck' when he was a Marshal in Abilene.[44] When Hickok tells him to move along, the fan becomes enraged and turns on him, saying he hopes, 'you're gut-shot and die slow'. Directly after this, Hickok abandons his work to play poker and drink. The sudden switch from admiration to hostile, murderous resentment points to a modern reading of McCall's motive for killing Hickok – the aspiration for notoriety. 'You think they know me in New York city by now?', he asks Bullock who nearly murders him in the improvised prison that is Mr Wu's (Keone Young) meat locker. But another reason hinted at is the combination of boredom and a deadly amplification of a personal slight. 'There's nothing worse than justified resentment', Milch has observed, 'it's like drinking poison and expecting the other person to die.' After Hickok cleans McCall out at poker he offers him a dollar chip with a patronisingly paternal, 'Go eat, Jack'. At this point according to the script, McCall immediately knows he has to kill him. We later see him in various modes of disarray; wearing a new suit with the label still attached, offering a garbled echo of Hickok's 'cunt' speech to one of his poker chums and complaining, with racist gestures, about the food he buys from the Chinese merchants. He's bored, and killing Hickok is a way of closing down the anomic, directionless and grim absence of occupation that we glimpse in these brief scenes.

Equally, McCall is a mirror for Hickok's more conscious decision, albeit narcissistic and grandiose, to die in Deadwood. 'This is my last camp', he tells Utter, and his forlorn companion pretends to ignore its implications. One reason for avoiding or never starting the work of settlement is the feeling that one needs to be pure before one can begin, that any False Step along the path vitiates the effort already made, negating the entire journey. In 'Self-Reliance', Emerson offers a sense of the costs of failing to live up to this:

> A man is relieved and gay when he has put his heart into his work and done his best; but what he has said or done otherwise shall give him no peace. It is a deliverance which does not deliver.[45]

61

There is an echo of the remnants of that fight in the chilling resignation of Hickok's final speech to Utter:

> Some goddamn time a man's due to stop arguing with hisself. Feeling he's twice the goddamned fool he knows he is because he can't be something he tries to be every goddamn day without once getting to dinner time and not fucking it up. I don't want to fight it no more, understand me Charlie? And I don't want you pissing in my ear about it. Can you let me go to hell the way I want to?
>
> ('Here Was a Man')

This is a craving for annihilation in preference to the failed effort of self-improvement or the torture of listening to the constant reprimands of a punitive superego. Hence, a moment before McCall fires the killing shot into his brain from behind him, we see Hickok pause for an instant as if he knows what is coming and allows it – perhaps welcomes it. This is the currency of annihilating self-loathing in which *Deadwood* deals.

Given his feeble 'Take that goddamn you', the moment of Hickok's execution hardly seems to match McCall's expectations: it is a somewhat underwhelming cry of vengeance and, for a moment, he experiences 'the dramatic inadequacy of reality'.[46] But for others, Hickok's death has a massive impact, constituting a traumatic moment for the camp as well as for the viewer. In slow-motion, McCall runs through the camp, pursued by the saloon-keeper Tom Nuttall, who pulls him to the ground, and begins beating him. Music swells, reinforcing a mood of mutual stirring of the camp, as for the first time, we see it acting as a single organism, converging around the killer.[47] Bullock and Jane, however, find themselves drawn to the site of the trauma rather than the killer, Bullock reaching the bar first, just in time to see Hickok's final death spasm shift his body from the chair in which he was slumped to crash to the floor. Then Jane arrives and, seeing the love of her life slain, drinks an entire whisky bottle, which while it drops empty to the floor, in another sense we never see her put down. Bullock's rage shakes the tears brimming in his eyes; the world seems to be shifting on its axis, hurtling toward barbarism. Another shot shows a Mexican on horseback riding into the clamour of the converging crowd, swinging the decapitated head of an Indian; the music continues to convey a sinister quickening of the evil elemental stuff of the world, its apocalyptic aura reinforced by the close-up of Andy Cramed (Zach Grenier), one of Tolliver's conmen shaking with the plague on his bed – as if the world were the hideous hallucination of a mortally sick mind. Historically, the killing of Hickok and the Mexican's return to camp with a head to collect Swearengen's bounty supposedly happened on the same day but *Deadwood* places them at exactly the same moment. Why?

Any sane aesthetic concerns the effort of art to interpret life, and the resonances that are activated by this juxtaposition of the decapitated head and the killing of Hickok, seem to want to connect with contemporary America.[48] The attacks of September 2001 which felled the monuments of capitalism were followed by a disastrous war in search of a meaning, the invasion of Iraq in 2003 and subsequent insurgency, whose bloody chaos was reaching the first of a series of climaxes as *Deadwood* was being written. In between the two, the release in February 2002 of the video 'The Slaughter of the Spy-Journalist and Jew Daniel Pearl' was released to the world, which featured his beheading. These associations swirl around this sequence, which nonetheless never becomes allegorical. In locating visually and emotionally similar traumas back in a moment of foundation in America, *Deadwood* asks us to reflect on the continuity of savagery, to reflect that the world is naturally, cosmically tending toward the same barbarism we see in the news today.

This is the moment where *Deadwood* seems closest to that other epic work of bloody history in the genre, Cormac McCarthy's *Blood Meridian*, a deeply violent narrative based on the history of the Glanton gang of scalp hunters in the mid-nineteenth century. But *Deadwood*'s artistic ambitions and worldview are diametrically opposed to those of McCarthy's; the television show is not an attempt like that one to locate and eternalise the violence of human society in a cosmic setting. Like *Blood Meridian*, *Deadwood*'s environment is thick

The Chief arrives in camp

with the particulate realism of the cosmos – the dirt, the blood, the shit, the vomit, the dust and the violent estrangement of men from one another. But unlike that novel, it asks us to see this immediate reality – of, say Jane and Bullock separate in the realms of their individual grief – as an illusion. *Deadwood* does not deny our alienated nature, indeed it depicts it with unflinching naturalism and the killing of Hickok brings us face to face with its consequences. The convergence of the camp as a single organism during this moment of trauma points us toward a view of human solidarity that the show will aspire to articulate as it continues.

4 The Primordial Camp

But Marlow was not typical (if his propensity to spin yarns be excepted), and to him the meaning of an episode was not inside like a kernel but outside, enveloping the tale which brought it out only as a glow brings out a haze, in the likeness of one of these misty halos that sometimes are made visible by the spectral illumination of moonshine.

Heart of Darkness[49]

It's a twenty-four hour camp.

Seth Bullock, 'New Money'

In his satirical essay, 'The End of All Things', Kant offers various models for the characterisation of the earth: as a prison, as a madhouse, as a cheap highway inn and, following Voltaire's version of a Persian legend, the earth as a toilet.[50] For David Milch, it is the Deadwood camp; as he says in *Deadwood: Stories of the Black Hills*, 'None of us want to realise that we live in Deadwood, but all of us do.'[51] What does it mean not to realise where we are?[52] In the disorientation of the post-9/11 world, *Deadwood* is a return to first principles, to a point of origin where the fundamentals of societal organisation are worked up and lived out. The camp is a petri dish where the beginnings of human society are restaged in an accelerated form, an experiment in fiction where the depiction of the ranges, limits and formation of adult solidarity makes it a tuning fork for the possibilities and nature of the social itself. For Milch, 'civilisation is a very young thing'[53] and the filthy medium of Deadwood's thoroughfare – a 'quagmire of piss and bullshit' – becomes the stage for the dramatic pursuit of what Robert Penn Warren calls, 'the secret worth of all our human worthlessness'.[54] This positing of immanent grace in primordial dirt reverses the dominant narrative trend in a lot of contemporary Western fictions which tend to offer the discovery of fundamental corruption and evil beneath the surface of normality, conformity and family (see the work of David Lynch for example). In those narratives, ordinary human relations are revealed to be toxic, abusive, symptoms of betrayal, degeneracy and decay. By contrast, *Deadwood* begins with these elements as the raw visible stuff of life and then shows how they are illusory dimensions of our estrangement from our fundamental connectedness.[55] The stickiness of the main street is the fecund place from which *Deadwood* grows its extraordinary characters:

> you have to sink the roots deep and then you just let the nutrition be drawn up so that the stories of the individual are nourished … by the situation that gave them rise, but you have to let it happen naturally.[56]

66

The master theme of this setting is the improvisation of society from scratch including a language which is 'continuously complicating itself'.

Visually the camp is rendered as 'one great blooming buzzing confusion' set to the music of the 'busy hum of men'.[57] It is a detailed historical artefact which provides a backdrop of constant motion to action that is freighted with the full density of a historical costume drama – the fabrics, textures, designs, architecture, calligraphy, manners, movement and objects of an 1870s mining camp. Maria Caso the production designer won the 2005 Emmy for her work on the show, and its prominence makes her a Gregg Toland to Milch's Orson Welles.[58] Along with Janie Bryant's (who also won an Emmy) extraordinary costume design (which clash, for example, Farnum's tattered and torn tweed and twine against the sumptuous silks and satins of Alma Garret), these artists build a textural sensorium which ravishes our view of the camp with a tactile vividness. According to Milch, 'by bringing alive the process of evolution of a society … it's precious to me to get the world right. The realities of a time are not

The busy hum of the camp

an inconvenience, but the door into its reality.'[59] Caso and Bryant's craft grounds the show in its elemental realism, earns it the frequent descriptor 'gritty', and it is this work that allows the show to track the camp's development as an improvised character in itself, from a tent-bound settlement of street fights and disorder, to a town with solid wooden buildings, a bank and a theatre – a place of emphatic and growing materiality. Apart from the ceremonies and events where the town converges – the killing of Hickok, the trial of McCall, the beatings, funerals, fights and wedding – it is always *there* alive and in noisy motion. That livingness is violent and threatening as well as gendered – the people who populate the street are men, prospectors, merchants, vendors, travellers, a slew of anonymity. This sense of the thoroughfare's masculine hostility is underlined when we watch Joanie Stubbs (Kim Dickens) wander through the mud in search of a place for her whorehouse where she seems surrounded, out of her environment in the midst of the recognisable signs of Deadwood society: sounds of fowl and livestock being bullied along, snatches of conversation, haggling, horse hooves, wagon wheels, the purposive but obscure movement of bearded men; lingerers and malingerers; the hustle and bustle of the camp's appetite for

67

Jewel's journey through the mud

commerce. A more oppressive version of this occurs when Jewel (Geri Jewel), Swearengen's disabled servant ('the gimp'), makes her slow journey across the camp to Doc Cochran's cabin – she falls in the mud amid the mocking taunts of the men around her. By the end of the second season we see Alma Garret walk through the thoroughfare toward the graveyard on the edge of town, but she is unruffled and confident – literally lost in her thoughts – and the town has become a familiar place (if not totally secure) although its details lack the visual focus reserved for her.

Indeed, the town is an attribute of the visual style of *Deadwood*, its signature tendency (as in the first shots of Clell Watson in Bullock's jailhouse) to shift focus within a shot from one plane to another to clarify or blur as a means of providing emphasis and revealing context (rack-focus). The camp functions analogously to this technique as a contextualising plane for the characters we follow and occasionally those background figures will snap into focus and claim their own space. The visual density and crowdedness is eloquent rather than fussy or merely content to display the spectacle of the past for its own sake. Instead the rich busyness of camp leaks into the edges of our vision; this is especially so in its versioning of John Ford's famous shots from *The Searchers* taken from a vantage point inside looking out to a bright distance. Edward Buscombe's account of that film notes that in those shots, 'the camera is positioned in a place of refuge, a dark womb-like space which offers a secure view to the world outside'.[60] *Deadwood*'s camp is more like a medium through which the characters experience the world than a hostile setting to be withdrawn from. Such shots are part of a palette in a repertoire of stylistic effects that describe and depict the continuing motion of the camp: outside, in usually bright yellow sunshine, we see the embedding of dialogue scenes amid crowds; shot compositions from the darker interior regions that allow peripheral glimpses of a busy world beyond; characters whose performances in their stillness, movement or gesture, cross the competing direction of movement and traffic around them; they all reinforce the overwhelming sense of change and therefore the need to adapt to survive.

It is tempting to see this style as emblematic of an evolution of television itself toward the 'cinematic', but *Deadwood* builds on an increasing density of rich *mise en scène* and narrative complexity already established in other excellent US television dramas.[61] It has the busy, chaotic backgrounds of *ER* (1994–2009), the walk-and-(sophisticated)-talk of *The West Wing* (1998–2006); the inky frame-absorbing chiaroscuro lighting of *The Sopranos*. Nonetheless, the cinematography is quite beautiful and unique. Particularly impressive are its rendering of scenes that take place during the liminal moments between night and day, such as the false dawn at the end of 'A Lie Agreed Upon: Part I' and at the beginning of 'Leviathan Smiles'. The pilot was shot by Walter Hill's long-term collaborator Lloyd Aherne II, but the majority of episodes were under the control of James Glennon, who also won an Emmy for his work on the show in 2005.[62] His painterly compositions do not rely on natural beauty for their power, but rather sculpt the light around the tatty man-made textures of the camp in order to emphasise its roughness. The sequences where characters are in natural settings are so few they can be easily listed: Bullock's mortal combat with the Sioux attacker during his pursuit of Jack McCall; Jane's treatment of Andy Cramed after Tolliver has

69

thrown him into the woods to die from the plague; shots of landscape when Bullock's wife Martha and his son travel on the stagecoach into town in the first episode of the second season. Nature in turn contextualises the camp; the green pines form a cycloramic curtain behind it which emphasises Deadwood's embeddedness in nature at the same time as it marks it as separate. For Deadwood is, at however primitive a stage, an ineluctably built, urban setting, its busyness akin to that of a crowded city. The show was shot at the Melody Ranch Studio in Santa Clarita Valley, California, the site of B-Western production until Monogram Pictures sold it to Gene Autry ('The Singing Cowboy') in the early 1950s; the lot was relatively self-contained, offering the massive street set with buildings and interiors as well as sound stages. This concentration of working space in a single location no doubt reinforced the sense of overall control that David Milch enjoyed as the showrunner (the person in charge of the artistic direction of the show and the ultimate authority for creative decision-making), but it also mirrored, to some extent, the narrative articulation of Deadwood as a place closed off and developing its own sense of rhythms, priorities and loyalties.

There were at least 200 background artists (or extras) employed to enact the roles of Deadwood's street realism; as Robert McMullen put it, 'They basically have us do "Deadwood 101" – just stand in front of your shop and sell something'; but the regulars developed sometimes quite elaborate acting business.[63] These mud-clad vendors provide a natural background of constant commerce, and yet they are convincing too as little emblems of individuality so that we feel any one of them could come forward and reveal a distinct human vitality. This happens to several background players during the show, notably Jack the bartender in the *Bella Union* played by Nick Amandos and Davey the *Gem*'s bartender played by David Redding: but the most vivid emergence from the background plane is Richardson (Ralph Richeson), E. B. Farnum's tall antler-worshipping cook, who is glimpsed in the early episodes and has a brief speaking part at the end of the first season when Magistrate Clagett's (Marshall Bell) bagman from Yankton, Silas Adams (Titus Welliver) needs a room. Eventually he is promoted to

Farnum's sidekick. It is the show that seems to notice his striking Old Testament looks and begins to pay him more attention, culminating in the various ways Farnum invents to dehumanise – (hence, for us, humanise) him: 'I imagine you foraging for berries and grubs, flicking at insects with your sticky tongue'; 'I imagine the pool that spawned you. I am filling it with rocks. I am holding shut your gills.' The more he describes Richardson in this way, the greater we cleave to him, so that his very strangeness is what we find we share with him in our discovered difference from Farnum's degraded, envious spirit.

The regularity of the continuous background of commerce reinforces the theme of 'settlement': our 'settling in' to the show and its characters as well as their own contribution and settling in to the establishment of the camp itself. Our deepening intimacy with them tracks their growing connections in the camp with one another. This convergence of the central characters is the work of the first season; it takes advantage of the serial form's capacity to thicken and complicate characters vertically – for example, in the revelation of backstory, and in their response to events – and horizontally, so that they intermingle, providing the dramatic opportunity to use and confound pre-existing audience knowledge of each one. *Deadwood* uses repetition to build character depth and deepen their co-mingling, and it anchors these to real regularities in social life: eating, sleeping, working. For example, the first season uses the restaurant in E. B Farnum's hotel as the setting for repeated breakfast scenes where many of the central characters encounter one another for the first time (Farnum himself leaves for his morning coffee klatsch at the *Gem* in order to report to its boss what he's heard and seen over breakfast). The first such scene has the Bullock/Star and Hickok/Utter teams meeting the morning after their posse ride rescues Sofia; Merrick, editor of the *Deadwood Pioneer* joins them, as he does on subsequent occasions; it is here they meet Alma Garret for the first time. Later when she takes over her care, Alma will bring Sofia to have breakfast here too, and soon after he has been recommended (by Bullock) to assay and maintain her claim, a cleaned-up Ellsworth joins them. Eventually he is able to say to Alma, 'I look

71

forward to our breakfasts.' After Hickok's death Charlie Utter finds companionship with Joanie Stubbs at breakfast after she invites him to join her at the table in the increasingly overcrowded restaurant, itself an instrument for calibrating the growth of the camp.

This radiating sense of community anchored to regularity is further reinforced by the Aristotelian time kept by the episodes, which is more or less consistent in the first two seasons, where most episodes begin in the morning and end at night. Often episodes end with characters about to sleep (as happens a few times when we see Swearengen and Trixie in bed together) and who we see waking up in the next episode – it is as if in the space between them we have missed nothing but unconsciousness, a reassurance that events in this rapidly changing place have not escaped our notice. Swearengen in particular is a creature of habit, pissing loudly into his pot on waking, enjoying a morning coffee (or is it that 'fucking black Darjeeling'?) in a china cup on his balcony, and reading his newspaper at the bar.

The consistency of the usage of time makes it available as a pattern to be disrupted so that, for example, the two episodes which begin the second season 'A Lie Agreed Upon', Parts I and II have continuous action. However, each episode is quite different in its overall tone: Part I is concerned with 'outer' matters – such as the spectacle of the fight between Swearengen and Bullock and the arrival of new characters, whereas Part II involves itself with 'inner' matters, such as the unblocking of the Swearengen–Bullock impasse, the recounting of Bullock's childhood, and Swearengen's literal inner pain (and the failure of Dolly's thumb to ameliorate it). The episode titles are varied and, like the music that accompanies the end credits, are extradiegetic creative contributions that nonetheless sometimes comment back on what we see. Some ('Childish Things', 'Suffer the Little Children') are direct Biblical references, others just descriptions of prominent events or themes ('Plague', New Money') or emblematic quotes from that episode's dialogue ('I Am Not the Fine Man You Take Me For', 'A Constant Throb'); others gesture toward literary or popular culture ('The Catbird Seat', 'Jewel's Boot Is Made for Walking').

Although these regularities establish a pattern where intimacy can flourish, the dramatic, disrupting events which beset the camp also function to stimulate allegiances and foster loyalty. Quite apart from the fact of the Gold Rush itself as primary stimulant for the formation of the camp, more locally it is the massacre of the Metz family that is the first event which brings hitherto disparate groups into contact – Bullock, Hickok as leaders of the posse and then, via the vulnerability of the injured child Sofia they are brought into contact with Jane, Doc Cochran, Trixie and Alma. The second event which, as we have seen, creates convergence, is the trauma of Hickok's murder and subsequent trial of Jack McCall which takes place at the *Gem*. This event flushes out Swearengen's sense of the congruence between his own business interests and the camp, since having a trial at all is a threat to its very existence, as he explains to Tolliver:

> We're illegal. Our whole goal is to get annexed to the United fucking States. We start holdin' trials what's to keep the United States Congress from sayin', 'O excuse us, we didn't realise you were a sovereign fucking community and nation out there. Where's your cocksucker's flag? Where's your fuckin' Navy or the like? Maybe when we make our treaty with the Sioux we should treat you people like renegade fuckin' Indians. Deny your fuckin' gold and property. And hand everything over instead to our ne'er-do-well cousins and brother's in law.' ('The Trial of Jack McCall')

Swearengen begins to align his own operation's prospects to the camp's progress as a whole; Tolliver on the other hand, does not have this vision – his view extends only as far as his own naked self-interest. The inadequacy of individual merchants acting alone is made clear when Andy Cramed, Tolliver's associate, falls sick with smallpox; Cochran threatens to reveal to the camp that Tolliver has done nothing with his knowledge about it – which would devastate the business of the camp if it spreads – unless he sends for a vaccine. Tolliver sends a young minion, Joey (Everette Wallin), to Nebraska to get some, but he contracts the disease himself returning to the camp a sweating, fevered wreck. It is

Swearengen who organises a collective response from the camp as a whole. The crucial moment comes when, in a move which bespeaks his adaptability, Swearengen does not continue to attack Tolliver when he discovers he has kept things quiet. As they both look at Joey, writhing in agony on the bed and being treated by Cochran, there is a cut to an angle behind and above both of them underlining the moment's significance:

SWEARENGEN: We should chat this all out.
TOLLIVER: Sure.
SWEARENGEN: Why don't we do something together? Us and several others.
TOLLIVER: Yeah, alright.   ('Plague')

This impulse to work together leads to the first group meeting of the camp elders in the *Gem* with the leading merchants and professionals of the camp – Tolliver, Nuttall, Star, Farnum, Cochran, Merrick and Reverend Smith. (Bullock has left the camp in pursuit of McCall.) Swearengen instructs a bemused Johnny to provide refreshments – tinned peaches and pears – a gesture which itself suggests a distant apprehension of municipal hospitality and responsibility (we don't see drinks being served), and the contingency of their presence is overwhelmed by the success of the meeting, so that they become a regular feature as a good luck totem of success. The group agrees to finance riders to secure the vaccine for the camp, and sets about the business of dealing with the plague – setting up treatment tents using the lot bought by Tolliver in Chinaman's alley; Swearengen displays a talent for adroitly using the press to manage public opinion ('give some sort of positive angle … looks like it's the mild fuckin' type'), while Farnum collects the money from the participants and hands out receipts. This depiction of civil society, however primitive its form, never loses sight of the self-interest of those involved (as Star later says to Bullock: 'Swearengen's had his hand on the tiller far as dealin' with this epidemic … the dead don't drink or chase women must be his thinkin' on that

The town elders gather around Reverend Smith after his seizure

subject'), but it also hints at adaptability that goes beyond this when Smith, who is afflicted with a brain tumour, has a grand mal seizure in front of the meeting. The group of hardened individualists gather around him, come to his aid: if the seizure does not exactly inspire a gush of brotherly feeling, it does point to a minute quickening of concern prompted by the extreme suffering of the priest in front of them; even Swearengen seems moved, noting that his brother suffered from the same: 'We'd make pennies off it when it'd come over him in the street.'

     I realise that, for some, my frequent deployment of the emblems of high art as registers of comparison with *Deadwood* may seem faintly ridiculous; but it is hard not to think of comparable achievements when we consider its figuring of character. There may be many other reasons to invoke Dickens or Melville or Shakespeare in relation to *Deadwood*, but the powerful claim is that, in common with the great works produced by those artists, it reveals the full, grotesquely comic humanity of these lesser, minor characters. One of the reasons we believe the background characters might easily come forth to occupy leading roles is that some of those in the foreground

75

The immense vitality of the characters

like E. B. Farnum appear to be mere caricatures. As E. M. Forster remarked on Dickens:

> Dickens's people are nearly all flat. ... Nearly every one can be summed up in a sentence, and yet there is this wonderful feeling of human depth. Probably the immense vitality of Dickens causes his characters to vibrate a little, so that they borrow his life and appear to live one of their own. It is a conjuring trick ... .[64]

This is true of so many of the characters and the wonderful performers who render them vividly that it is a terrible disservice not to treat each in detail – Jewel, Jarry (Stephen Tobolowsky), Dan and Johnny and Leon (Larry Cedar) and Con (Peter Jason) – but for reasons of space I've chosen one as emblematic.

E. B. Farnum does not develop or adapt much during the course of the three seasons, beyond a noticeable amplification of his strange blend of damp resentful submission to authority, and his abandonment (once he sells his hotel to Hearst) by his former 'boon companions' at the *Gem*. Apart from this he remains a weasel-like wretch straight 'out of a specimen box', a comic foil for Swearengen's cunning, not destined for greatness or even comfortable mediocrity. He is compromised by an intellect sufficient to achieve the awareness which allows him to taunt himself with the thought of all that he cannot be, to apprehend just enough to see the full cost of failure with the knowledge that he will never muster the resources to counter it. William Sanderson's exquisite performance threatens to steal the entire show (and it is a stroke of genius to partner him, in a Beckettian double act, with the compelling face of Ralph Richeson as Richardson); he carries the Dickensian sense of the tattered, vicious mediocrity of small evil. His strangled high voice is stricken with a nasty blend of fear and toadying supplication: no one in the camp likes him and no one ever will. He is universally despised, but hungrily welcomed by viewers thirsty for the eloquent depth of his resentments, expressed by his florid vocabulary (constructed, he claims, from 'a digest … which I memorise suppressing the authors' names') where we hear snatches of Shakespeare, the Bible, Wordsworth amid the 'cocksuckers', 'cuntlickers' and 'motherfuckers'.

Farnum's 'bailiwick specifically is new arrivals' to the camp, assaying their nature and value as objects for robbery, exploitation or

Mayor Farnum

77

partnership for Swearengen. As he says in a message to the sick saloon-keeper in the second season, 'A fish to rival the fabled Leviathan has swum into our waters. Get well soon and we will land the cocksucker together.' He is invariably described in terms that evoke unpleasant or feral creatures: Swearengen describes him to Tolliver's craps dealer and dope addict Leon as a 'Judas goat looking fella ... coyote type ... with his paws always damp like a just-shit turd'; Trixie remarks that 'Farnum's slithered his way across here'; General Crook's captain describes him as 'gopher-looking'. His oleaginous demeanour means he is rooted as an aspect of the camp even when he tries to distinguish himself from it, nominating himself as the town's first mayor and purchasing ridiculously ornate clothes – soon filthy – to signal his new office. He has the distinction of owning the show's first soliloquy, a litany of bitter resentment and grievance at Swearengen concealing from him what his weasel perception already knows: that Alma Garret's land is the site of a massive gold find.

Like Tolliver's reaction to the plague, Farnum cannot think far past his own interests and survival, and this ultimately condemns both of them to the misery of isolation and solitude. He comes to represent all that is blocked and feral about the camp: this is clear in 'Suffer the Little Children' when he proposes to murder Bullock and Alma in their beds, forging a note of sale so that his Team Swearengen can get the gold claim back. Al looks quizzically unconvinced with Farnum's bushwhacking scheme but their talk is interrupted by sounds of gunfire in the street – the riders have returned with the vaccine and news that the Sioux have agreed to negotiate a treaty. Swearengen now has to explain – for our benefit as much as Farnum's – why continued open violence and murder will not be the strategy of the future. It is like talking with a small disappointed child:

> E.B did you not hear the fucking news? Did you not listen to the fucking news? The plague's end in prospect. And so's peace with the fucking dirt worshippers. Come here, come here. Sit down. The dam has broken young man. And only ourselves can fuck up. For we are about to be swimming in

money. And how could we fuck up? By engaging in acts of open fuckin'
bloodletting. And right here at hand in our very hour of need, is the priggish
fucking douche bag Bullock who only wants to sell pots and pans, fan his
pretty face and hold his nose from the stench of our fuckin' sordid carryings
on over here. All the time thinking he can protect the meek and innocent.
The perfect fucking front man, and you want to kill him?

('Suffer the Little Children')

Swearengen's vision stretches further, beyond the current impulses
and into a future view of the camp and its stability. It is his peculiar
adaptability, his realisation that the clarity of violent resolution works
against the benefits of continued business and settlement, which means
the mortal consequences of the dramatic clashes between characters
can be postponed and contained, allowing the drama to continue and
flourish.

Because Farnum lives in the present tense of fear, and resents
the resentments that allow him no rest, he is equally tortured by good
nature, health and happiness in others. Watching the Titlicker – a
specialist Trick who frequents the *Gem* – Farnum murmurs, 'I begrudge
that pervert his happiness, I do.' But while he resents being used as a
pawn ('Al Swearengen's the cue and Farnum merely his billiard ball'), in
the second season we see him fraught with despair as his master lies sick
and unavailable. As he says to Richardson:

I don't like being weak, and I know that I am. I yearn to rely on a stronger
will. I fear what I'm capable of in its absence. Whereas you Richardson
know nothing of yourself. *[begins to strike him]* Are you shitting or going
blind? Or on foot or horseback? You vile fucking lump!

('Requiem for a Gleet')

Where Farnum's world of resentful spite is isolated and
confined (when we eventually see his living quarters behind the desk
at the *Grand Central* it resembles a hole in the ground such as a feral
rodent might keep as a home), Swearengen's expansiveness and interest

in human nature gives him an air of comfort in entitlement to the space he wanders through.[65]

We see him breeze across the camp in 'No Other Sons or Daughters', once again drumming up the camp notables for a meeting. This time it is in response to Magistrate Clagett's request for bribes. Clagett, who presided over McCall's trial, represents the legislature of Yankton and is emblematic of the external power that, following the Treaty with the Sioux, would allow the Black Hills to be annexed to the United States. But, in order to firm up their status as valid candidates for absorption, Clagett suggests the camp devise some informal *ad hoc* organisation:

> CLAGETT: Signs of conciliation and willingness would weigh in the camp's favour, but just as important is the presence of an *ad hoc* municipal organisation that would enable the legislature to say 'Deadwood exists, we don't have to create it. It would be disruptive if we did. The community's already organised, not legally maybe but certainly informally. Why not let's give this informal organisation the blessing of legal standing?'
> SWEARENGEN: What's the right fucking number for the legislature?
>
> ('No Other Sons or Daughters')

That response indicates his grasp of the corrupt underpinning of the abstract, political reasoning that Clagett offers. The paradox that the show engages with is how altruistic behaviour emerges in an environment of absolute self-interest. It stages the ways in which such forms of communal behaviour originate, develop and are initiated by impulses of self-preservation, self-interest and sheer survival. This is exemplified at the subsequent meeting to decide how the town elders will together collect the revenue for the bribes that need to be paid to Yankton. The necessity to show *ad hoc* organisation means pseudo-official positions have to be invented. Farnum nominates himself as mayor because he likes the idea of unearned power and status ('taking people's money is what makes organisations real', he says); Utter meanwhile gets pinned with the job of fire marshal, after turning up to the meeting uninvited but feeling, as the owner of *Utter Freight and Postal Delivery* that he *ought* to be there. Later on he has to act out the role, as he explains to saloon owner Tom Nuttall when he tells him to separate his stovepipe from the wall:

> NUTTALL: Why ain't you starting to talk like a goddamn government official.
> UTTER: I'm Charlie Utter that attended the same fucking meeting you did. And bein' they pinned fire marshal on me, I ain't seeing the camp burn to the ground. So either cure your stovepipe violation or prepare to get levied a fine.
> NUTTALL: Well I'll lick a bear's ass before I'd pay a fine to E. B. Farnum!
> ('Jewel's Boot Is Made for Walking')

Utter's hassling of Nuttall comes from his sense of responsibility but equally his fear of blame: it also indirectly leads to Bullock becoming Sheriff. Swearengen had already pitched his scheme for mutual tolerance to Bullock by arguing that, 'If the Treaty is signed be wise for you and me to paddle in the same direction. Tics or habits of behaviour either finds dislikeable in the other gotta be overlooked or taken with a grain of salt.' In return, Swearengen promises Alma Garret's safety from his interest in her gold claim. Nuttall, perturbed by the sudden rise of governmentality in the camp that Utter represents, pleads with Swearengen to agree to make Con Stapleton Sheriff. The latter, who was up to this point mostly a background player in Hickok's poker games, steps forward to lobby Nuttall for the job, arguing that he could protect his interests from officialdom. Once he is made Sheriff, in a tawdry ceremony photographed by Merrick, Stapleton is (off screen) recruited by Tolliver to murder a Chinese man in order to inflame racial tensions in the camp and thereby undermine the power of Swearengen's 'celestial' ally and dope supplier, Mr Wu. Witnessing this, and unable to suppress his instincts as a cop, Bullock rips off Stapleton's star and tosses it into the mud. Watched by Al at his balcony, he picks it up again.

    In an earlier conversation Bullock complains to Swearengen that Stapleton's corrupt behaviour degrades the symbol of the Law. Swearengen replies:

81

I want to tell you something about the law. Separate from all the bribes we put up, I paid five thousand dollars to avoid being the object of fireside ditties about a man that fled a murder warrant then worked very hard to get his camp annexed by the territory only to have them serve the warrant on him and he could take the six foot drop. Into the cocksucker magistrate's pocket the money goes, after which he sends a message, the five thousand needs company before I'm off the hook. I give you the law.

BULLOCK: It doesn't have to be like that.

('Jewel's Boot Is Made for Walking')

And in the next meeting they share a private ceremony, an anointing or marriage where the badge is restored to Bullock's chest and which is eloquent in the clipped rhythmic brevity that seals their synthesis as allies:

BULLOCK: I'll be the fucking sheriff.
SWEARENGEN: Starting when?
BULLOCK: Starting now.
SWEARENGEN: You have the tin?
BULLOCK: I do.
SWEARENGEN: Produce it. *[Bullock takes out the badge.]* On the tit.
BULLOCK: I know where it goes. ('Sold under Sin')

By the end of the first season what we have is not the establishment of Law in the camp, but the establishment of the camp itself as an entity under the purview of Swearengen. The final episode enacts the constitution of new loyalties and bonds of adult solidarity that characterised the first season as a whole: Bullock's rage finds a fitting object in his public beating of Alma Garret's father Otis Russell (William Russ), who had come to the camp to blackmail her with the threat of telling her family she murdered her husband. Before he beats him, we feel the camp converge around this anger – Utter, Alma, Sol, Farnum, Cy and Joanie as well as Alma are drawn by the gravitational pull of his fury. Beaten to a pulp, Russell leaves the camp by torchlight with General Crook's cavalry watched by Swearengen and Bullock from the

Gem balcony; Bullock wears the badge for the first time since the execution of Watson. And the final shot of the episode has Swearengen watching Cochran and Jewel dance, in the traditional emblem of human communion and unity. The camp survives the trauma of Hickok's death, outlasts the plague, and for a moment here banishes all that is hostile to its interests. Fittingly an anonymous deserting soldier swears fealty to the camp by baring his ass at the departing General; the camp is the glow that brings out the haze.

5 Alma and Trixie

Ah, love, let us be true
To one another! for the world, which seems
To lie before us like a land of dreams,
So various, so beautiful, so new,
Hath really neither joy, nor love, nor light,
Nor certitude, nor peace, nor help for pain;
And we are here as on a darkling plain
Swept with confused alarms of struggle and flight,
Where ignorant armies clash by night.

Matthew Arnold, 'Dover Beach'

On Valentine's Day in 2005, three weeks before the premiere of *Deadwood*'s second season, and a week after the release of the first-season DVD box set, Mark Singer's extensive profile of David Milch, 'The Misfit' was published in the *New Yorker*.[66] Singer had spent time watching Milch at work on the set and elsewhere, and his account describes the genesis of *Deadwood*, his research in the town itself, as well as Milch's own academic success and literary genealogy with Robert Penn Warren and others at Yale, and the fluctuations of his life as a user of various narcotics. Singer recounts how Milch arranged for a group of rodeo cowboys to come to Santa Monica for an expenses-paid stay while he soaked up the spirit and stories of their wild lives; he details Milch's writing method, of 'channelling' the voices of his characters as he lies on the floor of his trailer and an amanuensis types them into the script on a large computer screen in front of them.[67] In relating Milch's references to the Santayana, Shakespeare, Twain, the James brothers (William and Henry), the article alerts the reader to the depth of research, literary allusion and philosophical architecture in the show. It also anchors it to an auteurist notion of self-expression, here a process of mining the autochthonous products of exotic experience:

> Whatever *Deadwood* was about, the intricate self-propagating narrative that Milch continued to excavate each time he lay on the floor and looked into the computer monitor – all those strata of subtext and subplot – was so deeply rooted in his psyche that the cowboys [that he had invited to California] had become, at most, mnemonic devices. They stuck around [on set and as background players] because Milch … enjoyed their company or was grateful to them for helping to confirm what he already knew and in fact had understood about human behaviour long before he had ever heard of Deadwood.

While Singer offers a fine account of his history and craft, it is more accurate to think of Milch as a show runner, the ultimate creative authority but a central component in a larger process. In that sense, Milch is to *Deadwood* what Swearengen is to Deadwood: without them the place would not exist in the form we know, but they don't play all of the notes in the rich music that we hear; contrariwise, neither are they mere conductors or arrangers of other people's talent. Their presence is a necessary condition of the possibilities of each. By the second season, *Deadwood* has the foundations of its narrative and character as a shared history it can work with and against. As Sean O'Sullivan has written about the 'ontological fuzziness' of *Deadwood*'s second season 'as a place both new and old, and a place neither new nor old … as magistrates and commissioners from outside the camp seek to annex it, make it part of some older and recognised entity'.[68] This tension flows through the early parts of the second season, set in the spring of 1877, which shares with us the gap between the ending of the first with the departure of Crook's cavalry and the beginning of the second, with the

85

arrival (the first of several) of a stagecoach bringing Bullock's wife Martha and his son William (Josh Eriksson) both of whom he barely knows. In between, six months have passed.

In the final moments of the first season we see Bullock look across Deadwood's main street from where he is standing to see Alma watching him from her room in the *Grand Central* hotel. This shared look is full of desire; Alma slightly opens her partially unbuttoned corset in a gesture that signals the intimacy of their recent lovemaking and a desire for its continuance. It is a display for a spectator, and part of a repertoire of performance that Alma uses throughout but here it is meant sincerely, a true reflection of her internal appetites. More often we will see in Alma's outward performance an uneasy reflection of moods and tensions mostly obscure to her immediate apprehension. Our earliest encounters with her involve pretence; we watch as her husband Brom dresses in new 'prospector fatigues' for his early-morning outing at their gold claim while she pretends to be asleep. Her entire marriage is an act too, arranged so that her father could pay his creditors; in order to cope with the continuing deceit, she has become a junky, regularly drinking laudanum (a potent solution of opium). Later in the midst of quitting this addiction, she fakes being high on dope in a voluptuous performance of sluttishness in order to fool Farnum who describes her behaviour to Swearengen as a textbook case of dope-fuelled randyness: 'Lustful looks. Outthrust chest. The full catalogue.' Finally we see her marry Ellsworth, the coarse but reliable prospector first seen ruminating on his 'flatter'n hammered shit' life. This marriage too is one of convenience: it is arranged by Trixie to ensure that Alma's pregnancy by Bullock will come to term in wedlock; but having to endure an abortion at Cochran's hand, following a partial miscarriage, leads her to the consolation of dope again, which culminates in her taking a dose in order to gather courage to have sex with Ellsworth.

She is doubled and contradictory: at once a well-educated, cultured figure from the Northeast but at the same time a parvenu, who was trained in the false hauteur by her father in order to infiltrate that class as his surrogate parasite; Farnum's picaresque language captures it well as he supplies mining magnate George Hearst with a concentrated sense of her backstory: 'A haughty cunt. Formerly weak for dope. Most fundamentally a sexual peccant.' As is the case with many such adult deformities of spirit, their source lies in childhood, specifically her father, Otis Russell who arrives late in the first season and whose banishment from the camp is, as we have seen, part of its completion of itself as a settlement. His skills at lying and deception carry the implication that he is the originator of Alma's preference for deceitful performances. The cultivation of performance required to get the daughter of such a petty criminal into the upper echelons of society is, it is further implied, at the cost of her childhood – a kind of incestuous abuse which, although not physical, demands that the child stop being merely a child in order to be used as an instrument by the father. Effectively this is another economic relationship where the father as pimp turns out the daughter as whore. It is little wonder that she insulates herself from Deadwood's emphatically real world through drugs, lies and the performance of upright, uptight rectitude.

We get an early sense of her relationship to Deadwood as one of distance, performance and fantasy when we see her watching events unfold on the street below her window. When Hickok and Bullock draw on and kill Ned Mason, the road agent who told the lie about the Metz massacre, a cut to Alma watching from the window emphasises her excitement in witnessing this generic spectacle. Her father mentions her childhood interest in reading stories about Hickok. She is initially the woman at this window, confined to her room until Brom's death prompts her to the muddy thoroughfare to investigate, with a detached macabre interest, the extent of his head wounds. Her first encounter with Bullock then is through the emblem of artifice, the window frame, as she recalls when they first meet:

> Several days ago I watched you and Wild Bill Hickok support each other in a gunfight from the window in my room. Later, when Mr. Hickok spoke highly of a Mr. Bullock, I imagined it might be you.
>
> ('The Trial of Jack McCall')

87

Alma at her window

Although she does not seem to belong to it, her gradual living into the camp tracks in some respects our own habituation to its cycles, moods and surprises. Like Swearengen, who also enjoys a view from afar, she becomes an essential component in the camp's fortunes. This begins through a series of events set in motion by her husband's dilettante search for gold; once he is killed by Dority she is literally attached to the area because of her inherited ownership of what transpires to be a massive gold claim. Second, because Jane leaves the foundling, Sofia (who Bullock pulled from hiding in a hollow tree trunk at the site of the Metz family massacre) with her at the moment Hickok is murdered, Sofia becomes Alma's responsibility and an emblem of the camp's future. Finally, it is her growing desire for Bullock that keeps her and the child in the camp.

Sofia represents unalloyed good and her presence is mostly functional; she is a symbolic rather than a complex presence. In an emphatically conventional representation of the maternal impulse, the women of the camp – Jane, Alma, Trixie, Joanie and eventually Seth's wife Martha too – orbit around her gravitational pull of innocent vulnerability. She also provides an initial index of Swearengen's evil when he pinches her awake in Cochran's cabin and sends Dority to murder her. In the *Grand Central* breakfast scenes she is the nexus of attention from the avuncular figures of Charlie Utter and Ellsworth, participating in the latter's ritual of tongue-poking. Sofia is also a plumb line for the real; when Trixie arrives in Alma's rooms, sent by Swearengen ostensibly to assist Alma in looking after the child but in fact to keep her doped up in order to make her vulnerable to Farnum's offers to buy her claim, she immediately strikes a rapport with Sofia, astonishing Alma with her simple unmasked directness. Trixie gives the child a bath and dresses her as if the fact of being a whore removes the ceremony of manners in preference for the directness of sensual immediacy as the primary means of making contact.

   Trixie is a slight-framed woman with a loud, fast mouth whom we have seen brutalised by Swearengen and yet remaining loyal to him. Her awareness of the forms and moods of self-deception and their tendency to cultivate casual meanness gets exercised in her care for Alma in her attempts to quit her addiction. The expression of her soul is manifest in her brutal honesty, with no concessions given to decency, rank or status. While they share the common experience of being exploited by men and using dope, the distance between the East Coast Lady and the Whore with a Heart is calibrated in less obvious ways. Because of the gradual but prominent change in the status of women, primarily from passive biological objects and a source of unpaid labour, to active human agents, representing the most significant moral and ideological adjustment in recent human history, foundation narratives like Westerns designate a special place for them as signifiers of that change. In classic instances of the genre women represent the stable, civilising forces and threats or harm to them provide a moral rationale and justification for violent action. Equally they can figure as forces that threaten the domestication and diminishment of heroic masculine activity.[69] *Deadwood* is very careful about this, populating its cast with vivid female characters, and aware of the expectation that those women ought not to simply be objects for abuse; but it is mostly resistant to making them merely carriers of feminist ideas projected back from a

89

later time. They are often figured in caring roles – Jane at the Plague Tent, Joanie caring for Cy after he is stabbed, Trixie looking after Alma as she quits junk, and again during her abortion, as well as the wounded Sol Star (see below). Nonetheless, *Deadwood* is unthinkable without feminism not least because the depth and complexity of its female characters utterly overwhelm those of its male ones; it is as if the settlement of their interiority must come prior to the camp's eventual stability. Alma's decision to stay in the camp and cultivate her claim is crucial to the narrative shape of the final two seasons, but it comes at a cost.

Molly Parker describes her character as someone who comes to the camp and is 'reborn', but it is more accurate to say that she has to undergo a series of rebirths, or a constant re-attaching of herself to the camp as the bonds which keep her there evolve; Milch gave her a copy of Alice James's diary to read in order to have some sense of what being inside-yet-outside a close family might feel like.[70] It is worth tracking the contrast between the development of Alma and Bullock's romance and that of Trixie and Star. In the former case, their growing desire for one another is private and consummated subsequent to Bullock's savage public beating of her father. It is an elaborate courtship that ratchets up the viewer's anticipation through the accumulation of meetings, confidences and the growing intimacy between them. It is this that keeps Alma in Deadwood, a sublimation of her desire so deep that it leads her to suggest Trixie take over the care of Sofia:

> ALMA: Would you want to take the girl and go?
>
> TRIXIE: Where? I have no people anywhere.
>
> ALMA: You could go to New York. I could have my relatives there see you established.
>
> TRIXIE: What the fuck? What would keep you here? You want to fuck this man? Fuck him. Then think about the child.
>
> ALMA: Don't use that language with me Trixie. Or that tone.
>
> TRIXIE: Don't you want to say to remember my place? I do you *rich cunt*. And I'm going back to it.　　　　　　　　　　　('Bullock Returns to the Camp')

Trixie talking to Dan ... and to Alma: 'You rich cunt'

Trixie's 'just do it' sentiment makes explicit, with its crude spotlight of truth, the implicit currents of deceit and desire that Alma uses the weapons of class civility to hide behind, bury and sublimate; this pattern of conversation is repeated several times in the show. By contrast with Alma, Trixie is direct and explicit. In 'Jewel's Boot Is Made for Walking', she walks into Star's hardware store and asks if he'd like a 'free fuck':

STAR: Why would you say it that way?
TRIXIE: For Christ's sake Mister Star, my cherry is obstructing my work.
Would you take it from me, for free?   ('Jewel's Boot Is Made for Walking')

This directness is an avoidance of intimacy, a 'professionalisation' of the act, whereas Star wants to build intimacy – she calls him a 'Jew fool' for wanting to kiss her mouth, while clearly enjoying the *romantic* dimension of his desire for her. As with many of Deadwood's characters, Trixie's interiority, her deepest nature, can be tracked by following the patterning of her movements across the camp: from Swearengen's bedroom in the *Gem*, to Alma's room, Star's store and finally Alma's bank where Trixie works as a teller. The earliest pattern, established in the first episode, is her privileged place as Swearengen's favourite whore, allowing her to share his bed for sleep as well as sex; the episode ends with her leaving her gun at his bedside and climbing in beside him; the next episode begins with them waking up together. In the early planning for the season, Swearengen was to kill Trixie after seeing Alma insufficiently masking her sobriety on the way to her husband's funeral (she cannot trick him, even at a distance); this is adjusted to a scene where he interrogates Trixie in his office, violently gripping her pudenda as he threatens her, and as she reveals that she wasn't giving dope to Alma but helping her kick it. Instead of killing her, Swearengen does what may be his cruellest thing – reminding her that the life she glimpsed in caring for Sofia and Alma – let's call it the possibility of an enlargement of the spirit – is one she is not fit for: 'Don't kid yourself Trixie. Don't get a mistaken idea.'

Having Trixie attempt suicide rather than fall victim to Swearengen's knife serves to foreground her suffering rather than his villainy. She returns to his bed leaving, in the same gesture she left the derringer earlier on, a gold-streaked chunk of quartz on his bedside table; when he grabs at her arm to see the vein she tore in attempting to overdose, she strikes him hard across the face. The repetition is clearly marked by identical framing and camera movement; it alerts the viewer to the existence of deep structures of meaning held in the movement and actions of characters, while withholding the clarity of defining those meanings. The next morning, sitting by the bedside, Al discourses on his duties that day, the need to talk to the political representatives from Yankton; his tone is pedagogical – he is seeking to educate her:

> It'll be different after the annexation that's all. There's nothing to be afraid of. Everything changes. Don't be afraid.   ('No Other Sons or Daughters')

(In talking to her, he begins to reassure himself, perhaps discovering or inventing his mother's voice). This structure is repeated in 'Jewel's Boot' when he explains to Trixie that a warrant for his arrest is out on him for murdering a cop in Chicago just before he left for Deadwood; we get a sense here that his interest is as much in informing her about the way the world works as it is in telling someone about it. It is these moments that he refers to when he calls Star to the *Gem* to pay for the sex with Trixie:

> Don't think I don't understand, I mean what can anyone of us ever really fucking hope for, huh? Except for a moment here and there with a person who doesn't want to rob, steal or murder us? At night it may happen. Sun-up, one person against the fucking wall, the other may hop on the fucking bed trusting each other enough to tell half the fucking truth. Everybody needs that. Becomes precious to 'em. They don't want to see it fucked with.
> ('Jewel's Boot Is Made for Walking')

Swearengen is a creature of habit, and the hurt of Trixie's betrayal ('You sleep among your own tonight' he tells her after her visit to Star) expresses itself as a massive sulk rather than murderous revenge. Trixie continues to visit Al supplying intelligence on the actions and thinking of Star and Bullock and Alma. Ultimately, Trixie and Star will receive his blessing when he throws them a gift (not for them, but the gesture is eloquent) from his balcony, ahead of the wedding of Ellsworth and Alma that caps the final episode of the second season.

That season begins on a spring morning with Bullock and Alma having sex in her hotel room, while Ellsworth, who is in charge of shipping her gold to a bank in Denver, waits downstairs in Farnum's 'absurd restaurant'; Sofia and her tutor Miss Isringhausen (Sarah Paulson) (who we must assume has been caring for the child's education for some time while Alma has been otherwise occupied) join the guests in trying to ignore the 'song of the bedstead' above. It is one of the rare sex scenes in this adult show, one depicted in such a way to underscore its similarity to Bullock's rhythmic beating of Otis Russell's face. It represents a kind of savage annihilation that cuts its participants off from the rest of the world, 'a darkling plain', emphasised by the pitch blackness which surrounds both characters as they converse in an intimate post-coital moment. The intensity of this talk brims with the infatuation that excludes everything external to them as if the world is but a shadow to their desire; this is encapsulated by Bullock's dreamy response to Alma's question as to whether he is happy after they finish: 'I'll intend something, come to myself realising I've only stood or sat thinking about you – just now that your toes are beautiful – when I'd intended to replenish the kindling.'

Olyphant – here, as elsewhere, never less than intensely quietly brilliant – gives the delivery a shy sense of emergent trust and adolescent infatuation; Alma reclines in a way which precisely replicates the pose of Goya's *Les maja desnuda* – languid and voluptuous, but never entirely occupying the same shot as Bullock (we see her stroke his chest with her foot). While this is a touching moment in many ways, the only moment of pure happiness for almost *any character* in *Deadwood*, and certainly Alma, it is characteristic of the show not to leave the moment unalloyed. For we feel in the oppressive darkness that surrounds them, the insinuation of a pathological separateness: for Alma, it has become a habit whose sensual force replaces dope, while for Bullock, it is a means to channel the murderous savagery of his rage by having her ever present to him as an object to honour and protect. The plaster which falls from the ceiling onto the breakfast plates below as they pursue their individual

Alma in the darkness with Bullock

annihilation is a symbol of its wider destructiveness to the 'organism' of the camp. This is a way of avoiding being in the world, of faking one's presence which not only creates unbearable deceit but also destroys what has been built. This is made clear in the scene where Bullock tells his partner that he may leave town with Alma:

95

> STAR: What we've built and been through you don't get to walk away without saying why.
> BULLOCK: You know why.
> STAR: That don't mean you don't have to say it. I'm sick of knowing and you not saying.
> BULLOCK: I love her.
> STAR: Good, you fucking said it. And now I get to tell you you're wrong. You loved her these months and stayed. It ain't love that'd make you run but shame. Now let me ask you this: do you think shame would *end* once you cleared the camp.
> BULLOCK: It's shameful either way, Sol.
> STAR: It's *life* either way, *Seth*. ('A Lie Agreed Upon, Part II')

Star is the voice of sober reality here (although in a typical *Deadwood* doubling he is loaded on laudanum) pointing out that doing another 'geographical' – relocating as if the external rather than the internal world is in need of adjustment – would not salve the pain that Bullock professes in such a self-dramatic fashion. The latter cannot see that his adherence to an external sense of duty 'accommodates and protects him from the chaos of emotion'. The symbols of his poor vision abound; literally when we share his unfocused gaze after the fight with Swearengen, but also when Bullock, narrating in voiceover the letter he sent to Martha, says, 'I think you may laugh to see the mullioned windows with their view of the camp from out the parlour. Being unfinished they look like unfocused eyes.' While Star's clear-sightedness makes him a fine partner for a grim realist like Trixie, Bullock's tendency to theatricalise his inner turmoil through violence or despair is matched by Alma's dark proclivity to deceitful performance.

* * *

'Now I see what the fuck's in front of me and I don't pretend it's some-thing else,' says Swearengen to Dolly, Trixie's blowjobbing replace-ment, in a tone of abuse during the scene which ends in a register of what passes, in Swearengen's bed, for tenderness ('You don't need to swallow'): he's teaching Dolly now. And it is Swearengen who perceives how the Alma- Bullock infatuation undermines his plans for the flourishing of the camp. Seeing with clear vision versus the distortions of self-deception is a vital component in *Deadwood*'s design, enacted at the stylistic level by its repeated usage of unfocused and refocused planes in its composition of the frame. The first shot of Swearengen in the first episode of season two plays with our expectations and anticipation: it is taken from close behind and to the side of his head so that his curly, jet-black hair is in crisp focus against the *bokeh* of a light, indistinct background, a composition that acknowledges his iconic status – we know who this is.[71] As he reads out the letter from Governor Pennington to Adams and Dority we see him use a magnifying glass; he is long-sighted. Dismayed by the news in the letter – Yankton has established commissioners over the territory, not one of them drawn from the Hills in a move that is designed to plumb Swearengen's power – he grabs a bottle, drinks deep and steps onto his favourite panoptical stall, the balcony overlooking the camp. Telegraph poles are being erected just outside – unseen messages that cannot be assessed by sight alone (Swearengen will later adapt to this by befriending and recruiting Blazanov (Pasha Lychnikoff) the Russian telegraph operator to his cause); now drunk and angry he notices Bullock striding with typical righteous purpose down the street:

> He don't know if he is breathing or taking it in through fucking gills. They're afloat in some faery fucking bubble, the three of them lighter'n air – *him*, *her* snatch and his stupid fucking *badge*. … Self-deceiving cocksucker I am. I thought that when America took us in Bullock'd prove a fucking resource. *Look* at him striding out like some randy maniac bishop.
>
> ('A Lie Agreed Upon, Part I')

He publicly calls out to Bullock from the balcony, precipitating a confrontation in Swearengen's office. As Star tells Trixie as she alerts him to the imminent conflagration, 'Your boss should do like me – learn to look the other way'; 'Ain't his line', muses Trixie, reminding us that Swearengen's ability to *notice*, while a source of his strength, also makes him vulnerable to what he sees. For the latter, the matter is fealty to the prospects of the camp: does Alma, he asks an infuriate Bullock, 'have a going hard-rock concern and a five-stamp mill crushing gold out from her quartz all day and fucking night?' And yet she sends her gold to Denver, effectively neglecting what he calls her 'civic duty'; for Swearengen, the move on him made by Yankton means he needs Alma to invest herself and her gold in the camp, boosting its prospects. Bullock for his part can only hear insults; noticing the depth of outraged passion in Bullock's eyes, an incredulous (perhaps envious) Swearengen at his prefeminist worst, retorts: 'Jesus Christ. *Bullock*. The world abounds in cunt of every kind. Including hers.' Bullock's fierce protection of Alma is the pivot around which his violence acquires justification, meaning and clarity: at this point they are past words. The

97

epic fight between them that follows is described by Farnum as 'like some Greek battle'; by Tolliver as 'Gettysburg – fucking battle carnage'. It is a primordial mortal combat that ends up in the mud as they fall from the *Gem* balcony, Bullock landing on Swearengen, breaking his ribs, conveying a sense of primitive combat between alpha males, a sense repeated with even more savage ferocity in the final-season fight between Dority and Hearst's man.[72] Bullock briefly has the upper hand pummelling on top in his preferred style until Dan rifle-butts him, and Swearengen, knowing he has been bested in front of the camp, prepares to cut Bullock's throat. But here his vision shows him too much – he notices the boy peering at them through the window of the stagecoach that has just arrived in the thoroughfare; it is William, Bullock's adopted son – his face a picture of fear, curiosity and, in an inspired gesture, a half-smile. Swearengen relents, addressing the passengers with a jaunty, 'Welcome to Deadwood – can be combative.' As he later meditates to himself – facing the camera, face hideously smashed – 'Cow-eyed kid looking out from that coach. That's what fucking unmanned me.' The unresolved nature of the fight and the unexpected arrival of Bullock's wife and son causes a crisis in the camp that carries over to the next episode which is continuous with the first.

Claiming that he is not fit to decide, Bullock presents Alma with the choice of whether to stay and 'sever connection' or leave the camp with him. She talks through her decision with Miss Isringhausen, a figure who represents the externalisation of the retribution and rebuke she already feels. Ultimately she decides to stay in the camp, realising that Bullock's ultimatum involves her leaving Sofia, as he will have to abandon his adopted son (who inadvertently saved his life). This is on the surface a classic moment of melodramatic sacrifice redolent of *Now, Voyager* (1942) and *Stella Dallas* (1937) where a powerful woman abdicates her individual pursuit of love, her purported happiness for the sake of a child. In those films, however, what seems to be sacrifice is rather a deepening and enlargement of the spirit; in Alma's case it is mixed.[73] Giving up Bullock, like giving up junk, produces strange results: she prepares a giftbasket to deliver to

'Cow-eyed kid looking out from that coach. That's what fucking unmanned me.'

Martha Bullock who, in the aftermath of the battle, is with her husband and son in the hardware store, a gesture precipitating a dreadful scene of awkwardness. Alma discovers she has to work out the modulation between her private identity as a woman with appetites and desires and her public identity as a benefactor of the camp, someone who lives up to her 'civic duty'. Initially her choice to stay is framed in terms of petty revenge.

The morning after the fight, she decides to stay and 'sever connection' with Bullock, and accompanies Ellsworth on a tour of her claim, now heavily industrialised with many workers and large, noisy machinery. This seems to bring her suddenly to an awareness of her material power in the camp. She fires the stony Isringhausen, and decides to humiliate Farnum by offering to buy his hotel. She plays out the oscillation between being hostage to resentments, vengeful moods and forms of dissembling whose source and origin remain obscure to her, and a more civic sense of commitment to the future of the camp as a whole. In this way, she embodies and enacts a central issue with the nature of gold-mining camps: their radical instability. Mining for gold does not improve the land, it rapes it; it does not rely on seasonal change or provide hope for future improvement that would tie people to the land they work. Typically, once the gold is gone, the people are too. The very nature of Deadwood then, if we think of the town as a character, is that it is split between a yearning for stability, for the rewards and habits of stable social order and a fundamentally selfish recognition that this is built on the unstable availability of the gold that attracted people there in the first place.

Making Alma emblematic of this split therefore genders the history of mining and settlement in a surprising way: she is the means of settlement, the 'generative instrument'. As Milch observes, 'you can look to discover your identity not in the connection with the community but in the kind of radical "I" that will pursue my own destiny and fuck the world'. Alma's decision to stay allows the show to track this split between individual desire and civic impulse. She is at a structural level a conduit for the intermingling of the classes. This is most clear in her marriage to Ellsworth, a public settlement which binds the camp together in a raucous, musical wedding celebration. Her decision in the third season to establish and run the town's bank also contributes to the camp's strength and growth. But like Bullock, her vision is distorted, she does too much, believing her adherence to an external structure will suppress her internal conflict. Perhaps this is the only way civilisation advances. And *Deadwood* is, perhaps, more honest in its treatment of

100

Alma than *Now, Voyager* which has Charlotte Vale (Bette Davis) at the
end poring over blueprints to extend the sanctuary she runs. For Alma, the
ideal of the unconflicted spirit remains unattainable. Her weakness for
dope is seen by others as an opportunity to manipulate her; it makes her
vulnerable even as it further humanises her. In the third season, married
and established in the luxury of a new house, we see her staring out of the
window as Ellsworth plays with Sofia on the floor but she is no longer
absorbing the spectacle of the camp, but watching for the arrival of her
dealer, the scruffy Leon. When she sees him, there is a hungry quickening
to her skin, and she comes awake like a vampire scenting blood. We get the
unhappy sense that we can only live with the illusions of social convention
at a terrible cost, that the demands of modernity shred the subjectivity to
such a degree that only narcotics can salve it. We see her trying to initiate
sex with Ellsworth while she is high on opium; but her performance is
weak, and he rejects her. In a devastating moment just before, Alma shifts
the mirror opposite her bed, knowing that she might otherwise glimpse her
performance with Ellsworth in it. By contrast, in a later episode, we see her
repeat the trick of producing a coin from behind Sofia's ear that her father
used just before Alma told him to 'Get away from her!', a moment that
confirmed the history of their abusive relationship:

> SOFIA: Grandpa's trick!
> ALMA: It is, yes. And we oughtn't to let that spoil it for us.
>
> ('Amateur Night')

Deadwood's hard lesson for Alma is that habits can be broken, that the
meaning of actions can be reforged and renewed. She is, at this moment,
clear-sighted.

As partners to these complex women, Ellsworth and Star are
always clear-sighted and good-hearted and it is perhaps for this reason
that the show, in what is left of it, seems less interested in tracking their
lives. Ellsworth's goodness and his ability to read people as well as rocks
is not put to nefarious ends as it is in the case of other students of human
nature like Wolcott, Tolliver and Swearengen. Jim Beaver's performance

exudes a fundamental decency which seems to trip lightly across the coarse exterior of his grizzled face and gruff voice. When Alma, distraught that he has left the home after her clumsy attempt to fuck him on dope, descends her staircase whispering to herself 'I wanna be good. I wanna be good', Ellsworth is there to offer her the support of a kindness that comprehends and sees growth:

ALMA: The thing I did that made you leave last night, the thing I was coming home to do again. I pray now to forego forever.
ELLSWORTH: Not having me in this house is gonna improve your odds.
ALMA: I started using spirits at seventeen, Ellsworth, with no premonition we'd marry.
ELLSWORTH: Well, my feeling is that being vessel of purposes not your own, your eye was out for relief. But glimpsing since how being your own vessel is preferable, let the pressure off and you're liable to do alright.
ALMA: You are no pressure.
ELLSWORTH: My friendly hands will always be out to both of you.

('Unauthorized Cinnamon')

The monstrousness of Hearst's assassin shooting Ellsworth in the head is reinforced by the fact that he is discussing with his dog whether his late-night stay (after Alma was shot at in the street) 'disrupted the little one's routine'. Any world worth living in needs this kind of man. Equally, but differently, Star as played by the soft-spoken John Hawkes, is also a man fit to settle with. In a camp populated by outsiders, his Jewishness actually makes him a fairly well-adapted, conventional figure. When the camp is traumatised by the fatal injuries to Bullock's son sustained after he was crushed by a wild horse, Trixie goes back to Swearengen at the *Gem*, explaining later to Star: 'much as he's her misery, the pimp's a whore's familiar and the sudden strange or violent draws her to him'. In the final season, distraught at the murder of Ellsworth, Trixie tries to execute Hearst, but this time she runs back (after hesitating briefly) to Star and Bullock's hardware store. Now it is Star who grabs her and takes her to the *Gem*, in an acknowledgement and acceptance of the wider family; it is too a gesture that comprehends and accepts Trixie's deeper nature. 'Loopy fucking cunt', Swearengen says when he sees her, in what has become a term of endearment (only in this show!), as well as admiration for her bravery and courage. For all the writing about the show's eloquent depiction of masculinity, it is in the figuring of women like Trixie and Alma that it achieves depth and eloquence through its depiction of their fascinating and compelling lives.

6 God and Gold

For as the body is one, and hath many members, and all the members of that one body, being many, are one body: so also *is* Christ.

Corinthians 12:12

Remember this when you run your own place. That type guy hanging around gets people agitated. Forces 'em to take a position one side or the other. And agitation brings a slight bump up in whiskey-sales but the sale of cunt plummets. That's why I often wonder if I should take that fucking picture of Lincoln down.

Swearengen to Dority, 'The Trial of Jack McCall'

In December 2007, in the midst of the Writers' Strike that had paralysed the industry, David Milch was on stage in LA talking, lecturing and teaching writers about the craft in a four-day session whose themes ranged from the autobiographical, to the literary to the existential.[74] Much of what underpinned the content of these extraordinary sessions can be summed up in Milch's belief that 'our sense of separateness in every fundamental way is an illusion'. To illustrate the thought, he read extracts from 'the most successful writer that I know of', St Paul, including the passage from the first letter to the Corinthians that Reverend Smith adapts for Hickok's funeral:

> SMITH: St. Paul tells us, by one Spirit we are all baptized in the one body, whether we be Jew or Gentile, bond or free; and have been all made to drink into one Spirit. For the body is not one member but many. He tells us the

eye cannot say unto the hand 'I have not need of thee.' Nor again the head
to the feet, 'I have no need of thee' … . He says that there should be no
schism in the body but that the members should have the same care, one
to another.   ('The Trial of Jack McCall')

As he speaks we are given frequent shots of Bullock's uncomprehending,
hostile stare; we also catch Jane's inscrutable look from her vantage
point standing some distance from the graveside; and Joanie Stubbs's
self-absorbed expression as she joins the mourners for her own reasons
(perhaps for Andy Cramed, her friend, who has been left to die in the
woods). Smith's enraptured rendering of St Paul is flatly contradicted by
these emphatically enraged, estranged and separate individuals. As
Bullock begins to bury Hickok's coffin, Merrick arrives to tell him that
McCall has been set free, and the tone darkens further. Smith's grinning
smile at the heavens seems as much imbecilic as it is disconnected from
the emotional currents of the world around him. Bullock's glowering
expression tells us this is a time for action and revenge, not spirituality.

But Milch's charismatic account of St Paul's career delivered in
LA, well after the cancellation of *Deadwood*, reminds us of his earlier
intention to create a show based on Paul's time in Rome, where the city
cops, the *cohortes urbanae*, tried to function under the command of
the insane rule of Nero. Clearly, the origins of Western jurisprudence
in Roman law were an attractive theme to a writer who had spent
the previous two decades exploring the contemporary nature of law
and justice in cop shows. But perhaps less attractive to the fans of
Deadwood's apparent secular naturalism is its deep interest in spiritual
and religious experience, not only in its depiction of Smith, but woven
into the very understanding of how a society might emerge, even down
to the improvised religion of Richardson's worship of 'the god of antlers
and hooves', the genesis of which we see in his escort of Alma through
Deadwood's main street.[75] Milch and his writers seem engaged, like
much postwar American fiction, by the continuing valency of belief in a
world where the acknowledged secular register in many artworks was
that of meaninglessness.[76] Put another way: Milch was interested in

testing out the vitality of the grip of faith on his audience as well as his characters. But, as the scene at Hickok's funeral vividly shows us, preaching alone is likely to get lost in the noise of the world around us.

As Smith begins to quote St Paul, the arrival of the corpulent Merrick at the service is signalled by his hearty sneeze: *all* parts are part of the body especially, in this show, the gross, brute and indecorous ones. *Deadwood*'s first season seizes on the idea of spirit as an animating and animal-like force: at first the camp is a body where schism rather than solidarity and care between members is the dominant note. As we move through the second season the forces encouraging schism come more from outside. The sense of being a part of something larger for each character as they begin to cluster together is a gradual, ever-shifting realisation that accrues momentum in the acknowledgement of common purpose. 'Doing your part' recurs as a notion in the show echoing Smith's rendering of Paul, and reminding us that *Deadwood*'s take on the settlement myth is in its investigation of the way the psychological extremities of the social organism – the very broken and outcast stuff of the primordial soup *least* likely to cohere into organisation before murdering one another – can actually begin, admittedly in strange, halting progress, to shuffle toward something like the *grace* of adult solidarity.

Reverend Smith's manner seems childlike compared with the muscularity of the pursuit of self-interest that characterises the rest of the camp. He tells Bullock he got his calling working as a field nurse during the Civil War ('out of that crucible out of all that horror to come to God's grace'), and his cheery faith is cast directly at odds with the immediacy of dirt, violence, fucking and lethal mendacity which colours our early view of the camp, not to mention the sheer Satanic malevolence of Swearengen which casts a batwing shadow over it.[77] Bullock is a surrogate for audience irritation with Smith when he says to Star,

> The man is a lunatic. High water he never made much sense, but now he just utters pure gibberish … . What part of my part is your part? Is my foot your knee? What about your ear? What the fuck is that?

Deadwood then cashes out the thought of Smith's imputed insanity – confronting Bullock and the rest of us – by making it organically real. It is a cruelty of nature that his brain tumour will gradually disable bits of his body part by part – his arm, his left eye disjunctive with the right, eventually robbing him of the feeling of 'Christ's love', ultimately estranging him from memory, sense and, most catastrophically, the social world of friendship. In a repetition of the scene in the first episode when Star and Bullock told Smith about their background, he returns to their store, no longer a tent but a solid building. 'Are you Messrs Bullock and Star?', he asks. 'In the flesh' replies Star:

> SMITH: You are the absolute images of them gentlemen. But what makes me afraid is that I do not recognise you as my friends.   ('Mister Wu')

It is difficult to do full justice to any of the performances in *Deadwood* but Ray McKinnon's beautiful crafting of Smith's brave terror here is something to behold because it conveys that just enough of his wide-eyed wonder at creation remains to give him the courage to confront what must be the most terrifying thing in the world – the loss of a capacity to judge between the veracity of its appearances as true and good or as malign cover for manifold evil:

107

> I don't know what's happening to me. I have various ailments, and I suppose this is a further ailment, but of what sort I don't know. I'm afraid if you are devils which – which I don't believe you are because you were the kindest men of all in the camp to me. But if you were devils I suppose that – that would be the type of shape you would take and if you are not devils I – then I am simply losing my mind. And with my other ailments I am concerned – and afraid.

The scene takes place by lamplight, so that the low flicker gives just enough of a hint of menace to Star and Bullock's appearance to convince us for an instant that Smith might well be right in fearing them; until they gently remind him that they are his genuine friends by repeating their earlier moment of introduction: 'I'm from Etobicoke, Ontario',

Reverend Smith at Hickok's funeral; afraid that his friends are devils in disguise

'I'm from Vienna, Austria.' 'Wonderful', Smith replies, also echoing that earlier meeting; they offer to walk him back to his tent. This is a deeply touching scene that goes to the heart of *Deadwood*'s religious (there is no other word for it) project. Smith has lost everything, even his capacity to judge the reliability of his immediate sense-sensations; he no longer feels God moving in him; he is desperately ill, dying in fact: and yet he acts in faith, allowing the recognition of the force of the repeated

Preaching to Swearengen

moment of friendship to restore his social being. (The fact that the bearded Smith resembles the popular imagery of Jesus deepens the resonance of the scene.)

The incongruity between his holy appearance and the continuing filthy and brutal flow of the camp's business is emphasised as the increasingly erratic Smith becomes an irritation to Swearengen in the final episodes of the first season. He finds comfort in the sound of the

Gem's piano, creating an absurd and pitiful spectacle and mocked by the whores as he gibbers and performs to the music. Not for the first time we sense Swearengen's mixed feelings in his observation of Smith, even as he throws him out of his joint for 'kicking up his legs like a four bit strumpet'. It is, as usual, conveyed in the exquisite way McShane modulates Swearengen's tough attitude with a splinter of something else glimpsed, a deep sediment of feeling, not unalloyed or pure, but there. When he quizzes Cochran, for example, about Smith's prospects:

> SWEARENGEN: You notice too how he's starin' cockeyed? He was in here two hours ago, don't fuckin remember. *[the briefest of beats as he reads the expression on Cochran's face]* Nothing to be done, huh?
> COCHRAN: No. ('Mister Wu')

His feeling for Smith goes beyond the fact that his own brother had epilepsy. Watching him from his balcony, Swearengen sees the pathetic sight of Smith preaching from Romans to the oxen: 'thy circumcision become uncircumcision'. Directly after this, he pitches the idea to Bullock that the latter should become Sheriff. Afterwards, he watches again from the balcony as Smith concludes his sermon to the cloven-hoofed with Paul's rousing testament to the power of Christ, projected through his stuttering, fit-wracked body:

> Nay in all these things, we more than conquer through him that hath loved us. I am – I am persuaded that neither life not death, nor – nor angels, nor – nor , nor principalities, nor powers, nor things present or things to come, or – nor heights, no depths, nor any other creature, from the love of – of God. And – and Jesus Christ our Lord. ('Jewel's Boot Is Made for Walking')

As he speaks to random passersby he notices Swearengen leaning, drinking on his balcony and on the word 'angel' points wildly with his Bible at him; Swearengen turns away as if unable to bear the idea of being mistaken that way (a trait repeated often when we glimpse him concealing any hint of sentiment); it is the cut on the word to

110

Swearengen that gives the gesture particular emphasis, because the long shot of Smith's 'pointing' is just long enough to allow us to disavow its precise direction should we want to. As he stutters out the words, music from outside this world – a mournful, bitter group of instruments: guitar, harmonica, a violin – and the words themselves – *the power of the words themselves* – seem to keep the shaking man upright as he says 'and Jesus Christ our Lord'. At that point, Smith notices Swearengen above him and seems to recognise something or someone. Perhaps once more he feels the love of Christ; the reverse shot of Swearengen reveals tears in his eyes.

I suppose you would have to be insane, or deeply sick to suffer from distorted perception of such magnitude that you would mistake Swearengen for an angel or for Christ, or any kind of deity. But I believe it is part of *Deadwood*'s bargain with the viewer to test out that thought, say that a man so clear-sighted, so emphatically naturalist in his depiction, might 'spin against the way he drives' in ways that eventually bind us to him. When Cochran prays in his cabin for an end to Smith's suffering, remonstrating with God for his cruelty in the Civil War battle hospitals ('What conceivable Godly use was the screaming of all those men? Did you need to hear their death agonies to know your omnipotence?'); unbeknown to him his prayers are answered by Swearengen who euthanises Smith with a cloth, whispering in his ear, 'You can go now, brother.' The complicating of Swearengen is both an uncovering of that deeper sediment and also a transformation of *his* understanding and spirit.

The most obvious moment of Swearengen's rebirth happens during the traumatic battle with Bullock and its aftermath at the beginning of season two which leaves him mortally injured and blocked with kidney stones. His regular morning urination into the brass pisspot in his office is an index of his vitality, and even before his fight with Bullock he can't manage a healthy flow ('Age impedes my stream no fucking fear of you,' he says as he tries to piss just before their fight).[78] His blockage is a physical emblem of the impasse of the camp: Bullock and Alma's 'secret' rutting immobilises its growth, and Swearengen like the etching on the

111

cover of Hobbes's *Leviathan* feels their impurity in the body politic; their private desire is a paralysing as well as an annihilating force.

In the aftermath of their battle, his decision to return Bullock's badge and gun to him in the thoroughfare outside the *Gem* is a public submission to him; as such it marks a significant turn in Swearengen's thinking. Why does he do this? Earlier, Farnum made the same suggestion only to be mocked for its emasculating gesture: 'How would that chat start E. B., huh? *[Imitates Farnum's wheedling whine]* "Here's your hardware and as he looks a cunt anyway Al would like you to have this rose." ' Whatever the reason the reversal tutors the audience as to his changing form, as Dan tutors the confused Johnny:

> DORITY: Al's calling Bullock to the fold.
> BURNS: Bullock ain't even of Al's flock.
> DORITY: Al's gonna be calling numbers to the fold now that he can't trust like us. Some he don't even like. We're joining America. And it's full of lying thieving cocksuckers that you can't trust at all – governors, commissioners and whatnot. By God, that's just the new way of things. And you're just gonna have to get used to it Johnny.
>
> ('A Lie Agreed Upon, Part I')

Al calls on the past in a ceremonial gesture in order to flesh out this new way of doing things, handing his gun and badge to an incredulous Bullock standing outside the *Gem* flanked by an equally amazed Jane and Utter, acting as back-up: 'I offer these up and hope you'll wear them a good long fucking time in this fucking camp.' He reminds Bullock that it was Smith who said that he 'raises the camp up', and in the same sentence remarks that he was found dead 'some months ago'. As he turns his head to the side, close to Bullock he half-whispers: 'Remember the Reverend's half-dead face, that cock-eyed look like he was the victim of a lightning stroke, hmm?' We see that Swearengen, face beaten to mince and left eye almost punched from its socket, resembles Smith.

Deadwood takes the 'glow/haze' approach to meaning and such gestures enrich the associational depth of the show, in part by refusing to define or clarify in the manner of straight journalism. This is a point made explicitly as the severely injured Swearengen makes his way up the stairs to bed, pursued by Merrick who is hungry for the story of the fight. Merrick – at an early stage of his tutelage with Al – insists on Manifest Destiny as the grand narrative with which to absorb the untidiness of meaning and purpose. Al anticipates the scepticism of his anti-commercial idealism in his mocking comment, 'Whereas the warp, woof and fucking weave of my story's tapestry would foster the illusions of further commerce, huh?' Moments before he slips into unconsciousness, 'old' Swearengen delivers his final commentary, which becomes a narration carried across shots of the camp as he conceives an imaginary newspaper report:

> Tonight throughout Deadwood heads may be laid to pillow assuaged and reassured, for that purveyor for Profit of Everything Sordid and Vicious, Al Swearengen, already beat to a fare-thee-well by Sheriff Bullock earlier in the day has now returned to the Sheriff the implements and ornaments of his office.[79]   ('A Lie Agreed Upon, Part II')

As he narrates, we see Bullock returning to the home he built for Martha and his adopted son William – they represent the 'decent citizens' free to pursue Christian commerce. Swearengen is able to produce in his imagined story an allowance which satisfies both the understandable desire to appear pure in motive, while never condemning as hypocrisy the indulgence of other appetites that may compel us to self-defeat. The handing over of the ornaments of state is a public version of deceit, for Swearengen's power will be greatly enhanced with Bullock returned as his ally, as part of the publicly acceptable Christian family, rooted in the camp not on a 'darkling plain': that is the 'Lie Agreed Upon', the title of the extended episode that constitutes the opening of the second season. (That Bullock still believes in the import of his ornaments and that this is a childish thing is demonstrated by having him leave them in a little basket next to his sleeping boy.) Swearengen's voiceover seems to claim authority and command over the camp as whole, but it is also a farewell:

113

for the next two episodes he will not speak again and when he awakes, it is as a reborn, almost superhuman figure.

When we see Swearengen next, he is lying on the floor shivering and sweating in agony, unable to speak. It is a measure of their reconciliation over the season break that the anxious Trixie bangs on Swearengen's locked door, fulfilling her role as messenger, 'Let me just shout my information', she shouts, later keeping vigil on the street outside, smoking and drinking with Jane. When she tells her puzzled listener that Swearengen's employment of Jewel is not as he claims 'against having some hooplehead having only nine cents and wanting a piece of pussy' but 'his sick fucking way of protecting her', we hear an echo of his monologue to Dolly in the penultimate episode of the previous season where he reveals he buys his women from the same orphanage where he was abandoned by his mother. Appropriately enough the assessment of his moral character is subject to her economic trope: 'there's entries on both sides of the ledger is the fucking point'. Foregrounded here is the morally audacious calculation and realisation that the death of a pimp, a murderer and man emphatically beholden to commercial self-interest would be a loss to the camp. Trixie makes explicit what most viewers have already intuited if they have been paying attention. Swearengen – Al – is really not so bad; in fact he's pretty much the most positive thing about the entire camp. Given this realisation, the danger for the writers is to avoid constructing Swearengen as a coarse but benevolent patriarch – a kind of Pa Larkin who says 'cocksucker' a lot. The show seems to want to *study* what it might do with such a character; it is, like us, beholden to his contradictory appeal.

Swearengen's rebirth is offered in an appropriately corporeal and graphic manner with Cochran, Dority, Trixie and Burns as incongruous midwives to a urological nativity, as they set about preparing for the operation to cut the stones out. Lying on the floor sweating, shivering and moaning, unable even to crawl, he resembles a prehistoric beast just flopped wet on dry land from primordial seas. Cochran's probing with steel 'prick poles' the stones that block his bladder, causing him to shriek, a noise that penetrates across the camp, the sound unifying it. Once again Deadwood converges, this time around the agony of its philosopher king, who communicates with screams of pain and later, blinks of the eye. Finally Cochran, typically belligerent and wracked with fear as to his surgical ability, abandons his plans to cut open his bladder, instead encouraging him to piss the stones out.[80] The group lift him from the bed, holding him aloft as he strains to piss out the stones, and we see their white calculus plop to the floor under his raised feet – there is a hint of levitation here – amid splashes of blood. The birth metaphor is intensified in the group cries of encouragement, "There you go you ox-minded son of a bitch! Push at it you bastard! Push at it!'; each of them doing their part, Cochran with the sounding rod in Swearengen's urethra, Burns insisting on holding the smelling salts to Al's nose, while Trixie is told to 'milk his fucking prick top to bottom [to] bring that cocksucker down'. More urine, pus and broken calculi drip to the floor. A high shot over the labour bed shows the five of them as a single, many-limbed creature, another apparently contingent expression of the camp's immanent connectedness, sweating and rejoicing in holy grace after their efforts. 'Thank you for saving me', says Cochran.

115

(In order to indicate the transformation of Swearengen, from evil, self-interested pimp to a more benign suzerain whose interests are the growth and protection of the camp as a whole, despite his continued display of the mask of self-interest, I shall refer to him in the text from now on mostly as 'Al'. In his later conversation with Bullock, he explicitly rejects the accusation of an aspiration to dictatorship: 'What the fuck do we need a dictatorship for, that silences the public's voice and eases the enemy's way?')

Al now begins healing different parts of his body at different rates: Cochran informs him that, although his survival is 'a miracle', he suffered a mild stroke during the straining which has partially and temporarily paralysed his right side. Structurally, the episodes in the early part of the second season ('New Money' and 'Requiem for a Gleet') function to reactivate a pattern established in the first, where a charismatic character to whom we have loyalty and attachment is put in mortal peril and taken from us (Clell Watson, Hickok, Reverend Smith). Although there is much attention given to his sickness, this move effectively silences him as a power in the camp, allowing other characters, in a narrative 'rack-focus' gesture, to acquire prominence in the foreground, notably the arrival of mining magnate George Hearst's geologist Francis Wolcott, Sofia's tutor, Miss Isringhausen, who is revealed to be a Pinkerton agent hired by Alma's in-laws back East to pin Brom's murder on her; Maddie (Alice Krige), an older Madam who will partner Joanie in their new brothel, the *Chez Amis* and, to a lesser extent the figures of the livery owner Hostetler (Richard Gant), his friend the 'Nigger General' Fields (Franklyn Ajaye). Finally, we see the gradual building-up of the double act of Cy Tolliver's henchmen, Con Stapleton and Leon, as comic reflections of Dan and Johnny.

Wolcott is the major animating presence in this new group; he arrives at just the point when the camp is in danger of harmonious reconciliation, with the Bullock/Swearengen conflict neutralised, and he represents a new threat to it. He enlists Cy Tolliver in a scheme to destabilise the validity of the gold claims of the camp, harvesting the fruits of individual panic in order to buy them up cheaply on behalf of the 'Hearst Combine'. In this, he is assisted by one of the County Commissioners from Yankton, another new arrival, Hugo Jarry, who adds a legislative uncertainty which further destabilises the camp. Wolcott also reverses a con from Farnum, out of his depth without Swearengen's direction, also recruiting him to spread rumours supporting the doubts about the claims. It is worth noting that economic and mining tropes, metaphors and figures of speech abound in *Deadwood*, infiltrating the language and the depiction of interpersonal relations. Everything from Jane's 'I owe you a penny' for swearing in front of Sofia, to the frequently expressed idea of 'assaying his/her character'; at one point Farnum describes Bullock's meeting with Hearst as a place where the former will 'be dug at and sifted and shovelled until his crucial vein is exposed' by the latter. The suggestion which accrues through this usage is the sense of the alloyed nature of the human, our tendency to absorb the special objects of our interest and attention into our everyday behaviour and conversation. It infiltrates our very language. The show keeps coming back to the fundamental contradiction that humans are motivated by impulses and desires both obscure and apparent to them and the fact that gold is agreed to be a valuable thing allows it to act as a symbol around which such diverse behaviour and intention can be organised. However, this organisation itself carries costs, that of the alienating nature of capital. The thing that pulls individuals into communities is also that which finally estranges them from one another and from themselves.

      The first season is premised on the individual desire to achieve autonomy and fortune through the unconstrained pursuit of gold; emblematic of the deep psychological payoff is Ellsworth's 'beholden to no human cocksucker' speech. By the second season, we see him, as Alma's supervisor, escort her around her massively industrialised claim, with large machines stamping the quartz recovered from deep shafts and many workers scurrying around. As the mining shafts are sunk deeper into the rock so too the show seeks out the richer seams underpinning the behaviour of its characters. Take Al's remarkable visit to Alma in her 'office' at the *Grand Central*, where he reveals to her that Miss Isringhausen is a Pinkerton: 'I don't like the Pinkerton's,' he tells her, 'They're muscle for the bosses as if the bosses ain't got enough edge. … Bein' the Hearst combine and their fucking ilk got their eyes on taking over here, your stayin' suits my purpose.' This remarkably anti-capitalist statement demonstrates that his vision for the camp is broadening out in complicated ways, opening up to wider political and communitarian impulses although on the surface the claim to be motivated by personal interest is a mask he will continue to wear when it suits him. Equally, Alma suppresses her immediate desire for Bullock, reinvesting that energy in the foundation of the camp's bank.

      By contrast, Wolcott and Jarry (and, later, Hearst himself) embody a wider corporate manipulation of human labour: we never see either of them form friendships or more than exploitative or murderous allegiances; instead they spread deceit and subterfuge across the camp, exploiting personal loyalties and interpersonal friction for their own ends. Wolcott is played by Garret Dillahunt, the actor who in season one played Jack McCall; this coincidence points to a revealing aspect of his character. The casting seems to suggest that, starting with the same material, two kinds of outcome are possible: the degenerate gambler, rodent-like, dirty, ugly and motivated to murder through nothing more substantial than personal slight; and the handsome geologist, a wealthy, educated professional, who can read the value of the earth's crust, and serves a figure who represents such power that Tolliver and Farnum are forbidden to even mention his name. He is a product of Enlightenment philosophy and economics; when Charlie Utter protests at the way he has bought off the Manuel brothers' claim he shouts at him, 'It's all fuckin' Amalgamation and Capital ain't it Wolcott?' The latter retorts with the patronising insipidity of the well educated: 'Mister Utter are you a student of Hume? Smith? A disciple of Karl Marx?' Unlike McCall, who loses everything, Wolcott seems to be a man to whom everything, including knowledge and understanding, has come easily and without effort. Like McCall he is vulnerable to boredom, hence he plays at manipulating lesser creatures. Joanie's partner Maddie conveys this sense of a larger more complex organism toying with creatures beneath them, when she spots him across the *Grand Central*'s breakfast tables listening to Farnum's crude attempt to sell him Wild Bill Hickok's unsent letter to his wife. As she tells Joanie: 'the man the mayor expects to digest is going to toy and play with Mister Farnum for as long as he finds it amusing'. She describes him as a 'specialist' Trick, and what that means we find out later is that, like McCall, he is a murderer, a Jack the Ripper figure who kills prostitutes for reasons obscure even to him.

As a new form of (initially unknown) evil, he replaces Swearengen and his partnership with the friendless Tolliver further isolates him from audience sympathy. Wolcott originated as a way for Milch to get at the depiction of Hearst: 'Wolcott, who is fictional, came into existence as an avatar, a forerunner of Hearst. I felt that I had to know Hearst's child before I could know Hearst himself.'[81] The real George Hearst was of course father to William Randolph Hearst the

Jack McCall and Francis Wolcott

newspaper magnate, and the subject of Orson Welles's *Citizen Kane* (1941). Wolcott seems to have had the kind of minimal upbringing enjoyed by the subject of that film: all of the wealth and opportunity but none of the direct intimacy that schools the spirit.

The corrupting forces of Hearst's power are expressed through Wolcott as his instrument and, unsurprisingly, they acquire a Biblical resonance. It is a fact that the Manuel brothers registered a gold claim in

Deadwood in 1876; it was called the Homestake and Hearst bought it a year later for $70,000. The Homestake was to be the largest and deepest gold mine in North America, with over a billion dollars worth of gold eventually extracted from it. But because the ore in the Homestake was low grade, the only way to make it profit in this way was to own all of it and subject it to massive industrialised extraction. *Deadwood* adjusts these facts, dispersing them dramatically so that it appears by the third season that Alma's claim may well be a prize as big as the Homestake. It takes up the story of the Manuel brothers in order to think through this matter of the intimate social and moral costs of the sale on the primal bonds of the family.

We first see Mose Manuel (Pruitt Taylor Vince), a large, planet-like man, at the *Bella Union*; Wolcott's pitch to him suggests a depth to his grasp of the alienating conditions of the work and paradox of those prospectors who, exiled from wider society, come to Deadwood to pursue their fortune and yet need the communal resources of civilisation when they strike lucky:

> WOLCOTT: Do I guess rightly, Sir, that you and your brother do not deal happily with groups of men?
> MOSE: Nor each other.
> WOLCOTT· Yet you've made a rich find and done very well in beginning its development.
> MOSE: State your business.
> WOLCOTT: Further development may require organisation on a scale and dealings with men to which you and your brother are not suited or disposed to attempt.
> MOSE: With thieving bastard Cornishmen you mean. Underground in the shafts, high-graders every one of them. ('Childish Things')

The organisation of labour requires patience and the assertion of sometimes brutal authority; but there are those like Manuel who are barely able to participate in any social interaction, not even with his brother Charlie who he claims has 'encumbered every fuckin' breath

I've ever fucking taken' but who must agree to the sale in order for it to be legitimate. As Mose goes off to find the saloon his brother is in, in order to convince him, the scene shifts to one of *Deadwood*'s greatest spectacles of spontaneous organic unity, Tom Nuttall's bike ride through the camp. Earlier in the episode we saw this camp pioneer saloon-keeper take delivery of an unwieldy-looking 'boneshaker', and now, to counter the mocking of his drunken clientele, he boasts: 'My bicycle masters boardwalk and quagmire with aplomb! Those that doubt me suck cock by choice!' Many bets are taken and the news travels that Tom will attempt to ride down the thoroughfare without falling off. The lightness of this event lifts the entire camp, which converges cheering around his bumpy journey – Al on his balcony (offering a very British, 'Go on, my Son!'), and even Wolcott is caught up in the spirit of it, a brief but broad grin escaping him as he is jostled by the crowd celebrating Tom's triumph.[82] (Sheriff Bullock even grins at 'Soapy' [Gill Gayle] the street hustler who is usually his constant irritant and target for rebuke when in a mean mood.) These events colour the one we see intercut with the bang of the starting shotgun as an act of deepest private villainy: Mose shooting his brother with a pistol in Tom's empty bar. Later, Wolcott collaborates in the destruction of Charlie's body using his Chinese henchman from San Francisco, Mr Lee (Philip Moon), to burn the remains. Despite his new wealth, which allows Mose to gorge on expensive food, drink and Tess (Parisse Boothe), presumably the *Bella Union*'s most expensive whore, he balks at it: one imagines the very intensity of sensual reward is only a vivid reminder of the terrible nature of fratricide. As Charlie Utter correctly predicts to Bullock when they attempt to investigate the death, Mose eventually becomes 'judge on hisself' and demands: 'I want it back! All of it!' Wolcott rounds on him with the scalpel-like viciousness of a sadistic therapist:

121

> Including youth, Mister Manuel? And why not beauty? Not credibly restored, perhaps, but as a new non-negotiable term? Would you not have, too, your brother Charlie resurrected? Would you stipulate your envy of him be purged? Surely you'll insist that Charlie retain certain defects – his ineffable self-deceptions, for example, which were your joy in life to

The camp converges again: Nuttall's bike ride

> rebuke, and purpose, so far as you had one. I suppose you would see
> removed those qualities which caused you to love him, and the
> obliviousness to danger which allowed you to shed his blood.
>
> ('Amalgamation and Capital')

As Manuel raises his pistol to silence this devilish analysis, he is shot
by Tolliver's cappers, then carted off on a sled, barely alive. Wolcott's
interest in the shattered psychology of those he deems beneath him
makes him an efficient instrument for the Hearst combine. When he
tells Mose during his pitch for the claim, that they know how to 'deal
effectively' with high grading we already know the brutal resonance
of the phrase. The episode begins with Wolcott composing a letter to
Hearst and, as he does so, a voiceover relays his words over a scene of
the Hearst minehead. The sequence deliberately evokes imagery of Nazi
death camps: we see naked men showering under the supervision of
armed guards as Wolcott's voice continues:

> until workers at wage outnumber individual prospectors in the camp, the
> matter of Chinese labour remains delicate of introduction and we must

therefore rest content with Germans and Cornish unwilling to work at night. We shower them after every shift, and the gold they've combed into their hair with grease we recover from the traps installed beneath the wash-house facility … through the vigilance of our security fellows, the unremitting larceny of these cunning and clannish men is held somewhat in check. I cite in particular the effectiveness of Captain Turner, invaluable to us since the Comstock.[83]   ('Childish Things')

We see one naked miner, after having a nugget removed from his rectum, attempt to flee and be killed, shot in the back by Turner (Alan Graf). This nightmarish scene in a location grey and wet is in contrast to the sunny shots of the Garret claim, where we observe supervisor Ellsworth discussing with his friendly dog whether he should propose to Alma. Indeed, our introduction to Wolcott is coloured by Ellsworth's hostility to him when he wanders onto Alma's claim, describing him as 'bloodied from the Comstock' (Wolcott's reply indicates Ellsworth's heroic role in a mining disaster). As he leaves, he gestures to the loud noise of the quartz stamping machines: 'The noise is terrible, isn't it Mister Ellsworth? Like fate.' In these terms, the fate of the world, its oncoming modernity, is mechanical, like an apparatus, unyielding to

123

Burning the Chinese girls

human need or pity; Swearengen puts the stakes clearly to Bullock in terms that situate the oddity of their natures against the implacable 'murderous engine' of Hearst:[84]

> 'Our cause is surviving, not bein' allied with Yankton or cogs in the Hearst machine, to show it don't fate us as runts, or two-headed calves or pigs with excess legs, to a good fuckin' grindin' up.' ('Childish Things')

Al's language captures the sense of the deformed organic against the machine. This figuring of mass industrial organisation as a form of technological dehumanisation, as inimical to the spirit, is a fairly conventional trope; but *Deadwood* recruits these notions to a novel end by investigating the reasons why human beings might *want* to be enslaved, consciously or not, by such a machine. It does so through the depiction of the brutality of prostitution. In the second explicit reference to the Holocaust we see Wolcott and Lee organise the arrival of trucks of young Chinese whores (some of whom seem very young) and who are to be, in Milch's words, 'fucked to death'; later we see their flimsy childlike corpses being tossed onto a pyre, the stench of the burning drifting across the camp.[85] As with Al's shrieks, it is another deeply distubing way the camp is unified. Can women be treated with impunity in this way and the idea of God continue?

124

7 Cy and Joanie

There are moods in which we court suffering, in the hope that here, at least, we shall find reality, sharp peaks and edges of truth. But it turns out to be scene-painting and counterfeit.

Emerson, 'Experience'[86]

Help me understand cunt, Lord.

Cy Tolliver, 'Tell Him Something Pretty'

I have pointed to *Deadwood*'s technique of changing the plane of focus within a shot as a stylistic signature of the show; it is used to direct attention, to establish relations between foreground and background, and otherwise contextualise what was in focus and now blurred, with what was before less defined, and now clear. It is also a technique which, in avoiding the cut or camera movement, seems to locate intentionality and meaning much more within the composition and balance of the frame, a thought that emerges in the image. These moments are expressive of the show's placing things – say, faces and people and their actions – in context, and making the context in which we find them significant. It is the thing that brings their individualities out in relief but also blends them into a world. The technique can isolate but also situate or settle the isolated thing in its place; it is a style that is congruent with the show's overall thematic interest in finding a place for each character to 'do their part'. Equally, the movement of the characters within the world of *Deadwood* alternates between their isolation and their being bound into the dramas and conflicts of that place and with one another. Characters have their familiar homes, the places they've settled in and yet, for *Deadwood*'s project of intermingling humanity to work, they have to move as well.

Doc Cochran exemplifies this dynamic, guarding the privacy of his cabin, which looks like part of the forest with its walls of broad pine trunks and hanging herb roots, yet we also find him abroad in his capacity of providing regular maintenance for what Jane describes as 'them whore's business areas'; he has found a way to accommodate the defects of his character in a professional role, which allows him to express his belligerent irritation with people with impunity. He is an individual, sharply cut out from the background and yet also a type – the ornery medico; like his curly hair, in close-up he is all prickles and wiriness; but he is something that can blend and blur in happy, kind, ways.[87] Although we see him in furious despair at God's neglect of (or, by another light, attention to) Reverend Smith's pain, and in truculent vexation with Al, his moments of delight in those medical recoveries he is responsible for – Mose Manuel, Alma and Al – lift us too because we glimpse his availability to relief from constant irritation. Equally, because like Charlie Utter he seems to be 'the camp's conscience' and moral analyst (in so far as both have a sense of moral anchoring), we are interested in his assessment of others. When he says to Al that 'you generate [your moods] yourself and then find your excuse for having them' or in his depiction of Alma's offer to send Trixie with Sofia to New York as a 'cruel masquerade', we can acknowledge the acuity of his observation. Following Cochran's movements, we get a sense of the insistent gravity of suffering in the camp and his being pulled to respond to it despite his fear of doing further harm. He is a moral weathervane, fashioning a boot for Jewel, and treating the whores with quiet, irritable deliberation. This is manifest in the sequence where he refuses to operate on the wounded Mose Manuel, returning instead to the cabin where the mortally injured William Bullock lies dying; on seeing Martha and Seth clutched around the child through the window, he goes back to attempt the surgery. And he manages to save this large but babylike creature, as

Cochran: 'Leave the demons to God and trust the pain to me.'

if saving him atones for the terrible death of William, whose funeral too, christens a kind of moral growth in the camp.[88] Cochran is an emblem of the possibility of goodness surviving in a camp at all, someone who cannot be bought off.

These qualities mean he can speak truth to Evil. His conversation with the vile misogynist pimp/boss of the *Bella Union*, Cy Tolliver, when he offers to treat the Chinese whores that Wolcott and Mr Lee have imported to the camp, illustrates the way his treatment of the sick is an aspect of his deepest moral nature:

> COCHRAN: I'd be available to see to their care like I do these here.
> TOLLIVER: Declined with thanks.
> COCHRAN: You may not be aware that beyond their afflictions these girls are *fucking starving to death*!
> TOLLIVER: I ain't one Doc, holds the white man's as the sole and only path. I strive to tolerate what I may not agree with. But those people's culture, their women are disposable. They ship 'em unfed, replace them when they expire. They dose them with opium which I gather eases their pangs.   ('Childish Things')

127

This turning out of the evil racism of Tolliver's relativism, his 'respect' for cultural diversity, is characteristic of *Deadwood*'s interest in the ethnic sin at the heart of the formation of America (which I shall return to in the next chapter). Cochran's furious moral resistance – 'I have to live too' – points also to the seam of human virtue that balks at such horror.

Powers Boothe provides a haunting, beautiful, performance as a tough boss who is both evil and pitiful, but one who lacks Swearengen's lived commitment to the camp beyond his own interests; instead the thing he has beyond himself is his love for Joanie. When it arrives in the camp, the upmarket *Bella Union* team with its 'fancy signs and cleaned-up women' seems to be an organised, well-drilled threat to Al's shabbier, improvised *Gem* operation. Tolliver's chief dealer and cardsharp Eddie Sawyer is played with winning kindness by the magician Ricky Jay, and Joanie Stubbs exudes professionalism as whoremistress in charge of providing high-class atmosphere, baiting new marks to be hustled and cheated (we see her in action with Ellsworth). Tolliver's aspirations to a higher class of exploitation are evident in the decoration of the *Bella Union*, especially the tastefully erotic painting on the staircase, perhaps a gesture to bourgeois refinement. Swearengen, on the other hand, has a photo of Lincoln in the bar and what looks like porn on his office wall. While Swearengen and Tolliver live out the rest of their time in the show as rivals they are never direct enemies in conflict; instead these two power blocs are best understood in the way *Deadwood* presents them, as dysfunctional families whose members orbit around powerful but flawed patriarchs.

Al's family is based on loyalty and the authority of violence in the service of his deep strategic and tactical agility; Dority is fiercely loyal to Al like an elder son, breaking down and weeping when the latter appears to favour Silas Adams in a dispute; he will fight to the death with Hearst's second, the monstrous Captain Turner. Adams himself is an adopted son, taken in by Al as a student and potential successor; we see the narrative of him joining the family as a matter of choice, slitting Magistrate Clagett's throat while looking into Al's eyes in a gruesome gesture of fealty. Finally, Johnny Burns is the younger, dim-witted but good-hearted child, eager to please but without the capacity or maturity for reliable independent action. On a more distant orbit, E. B. Farnum, Mr Wu and Doc Cochran complete this homosocial portrait of loyal staff struggling to keep up with superior leadership and thought. Trixie, once offered leave to 'sally forth', finds companionship with Star but returns to her 'familiar', as she calls her pimp, to provide information, counsel and encouragement. It is an expansive and inclusive family, eager to incorporate and welcome in. By the final episodes, with Alma shot at by Hearst's hired mercenaries, the *Gem* becomes a place of refuge and gathering with Bullock, Alma, Sofia and others converging within.

By contrast, Tolliver's *Bella Union* in the final episode is virtually empty; his family is restricted and exclusive and we get a sense of a suffocating clash of moods, resentments and grievances toward a patriarch who visits untempered pathologies on his nervous brood. We don't learn the reasons the crew has moved from its gambling operation on 'the river', but it is not long before Cy begins to destroy his 'family': first, he abandons their plague-stricken partner Andy Cramed in the forest to die alone; when he survives and returns to camp reborn as a minister, Tolliver repeatedly taunts his faith, describing him as a plague infecting his whores with 'bible-talk', and provoking Cramed to gut-stab him in the street. Once Eddie and Joanie leave him, his only loyal crew consists of the double act of flaky dope addict Leon and blustering cardsharp Con Stapleton; when Tolliver is looking for a second to match Swearengen's appointment of Adams as his intermediary in discussions with Hearst, he discovers Con playing with the large breasts of a whore in a bathtub: 'I'd need to know my man had discipline and appetites in fucking harness', he says as Con looks vacantly on – a bizarre comic moment that only reinforces our sense of Tolliver as a man who has not been able to cultivate his staff as useful instruments for his purposes. In part this is because his own appetites are not properly 'in harness'.

We see this in the first season when, in a further emblem of his destruction of families, he stages the torture and killing of two young thieves, Flora (Kristen Bell) and Miles (Greg Cipes), who infiltrate the camp. Flora is befriended by Joanie, who tutors her in the arts of

129

'Don't believe there's no good women till you seen one with maggots in her eyes.'

whoredom; importantly, their cover story is that they are in camp
searching for their lost father – Tolliver cracks on to the act before
Joanie, whose relationship with Flora reveals a yearning for female
companionship that stems from her abused childhood. After Flora tries
to rob Joanie's jewels, the pair are captured and viciously beaten.
Tolliver puts them in Joanie's room and acts out a violent psychodrama
which mirrors as well as reveals his complex dependence on, and shame
about, his love for Joanie:

> TOLLIVER: *[to the bloodied Miles lolling semiconscious in a chair]* Don't be
> fucking passing out youngster. Next fucking breath you draw the smell of
> fucking sulfur's liable to be strong in your nose. *Where is your fucking nose,*
> *anyway?* Fuck it, Miles! You're found guilty of being a *cunt.* I'm hereby
> passing judgment for you letting this little bitch push you around and
> telling you what to do. When you were supposed to be a man and showing
> her the fucking rules! ('Suffer the Little Children')

He shoots Miles and hands the gun to Joanie telling her to 'put that out
of its misery'; she kills Flora and, not for the last time, puts the gun to

her own head. Tolliver stops her, but the brutal cruelty of the killings in such an intimate space finally breaks up the team. Eddie Sawyer, also forced to witness it, begins to rob Tolliver in order to fund the brothel he promises Joanie as a way of placating her traumatised misery after the murders. Why is Tolliver the way he is with her?

In what at first sight seems an odd gesture, after Alma's father has been beaten to a pulp by Bullock at the end of season one, Joanie brings her some of his bloodied teeth wrapped in a handkerchief. In support of Alma's mixed feelings, Joanie recounts how she came to work for Cy, how, once her mother died of cholera, her father convinced her to 'see to his needs' and 'add to the egg money' by getting her to convince her sisters to 'seeing to his needs and then to the men … 'til he sold me to Cy Tolliver'. As the latter tells Maddie, Joanie's older partner at the *Chez Amis*, since she was fourteen he has been giving her jewels 'for her fuck money' (the jewels Flora tries to steal). This, and the caring way she inducts Flora allows us to see the fact of prostitution, from the well-dressed whores in the *Chez Amis* and *Bella Union* to the ragged ones in the *Gem*, as all versions of the caged slavery we see the Chinese whores suffer. Joanie and Cy's twisted relationship represents a strand of the show's interest in the social and psychological consequences of such brutal indenture. There are gradations to slavery, ranging from Alma being trained by her father to occupy the social elite in order to pay off his debts, to the blatant display of imprisonment and starvation of the Chinese women. When Al is tutoring Bullock in the ways of the world, he gestures to a passing *Gem* whore and tells Bullock, 'Look at her. You know she's fucked for food.' Perhaps we notice the one he points to is Dolly, who has replaced Trixie as chief sucker of his cock, a girl who is clearly, sweetly, in love with him. Or take Con Stapleton's attempt to pitch the novelty of the new Chinese whores to the denizens of the *No. 10 Saloon*, as having 'an ancient way of milking ya of yer sorrow and ya loneliness and that awful feeling of being forsaken', a description whose accuracy seems to stun its tatty male audience to silent reflection. Such matters are the currency of *Deadwood*'s artistic economy; it troubles the secure

131

vantage of hygienic morality and challenges us to wonder if there can be a world where no human is used instrumentally.

What makes Tolliver distinct from Al is the internal economy of shame provoked by his awareness of his love for Joanie: it unmans him and drives a corresponding compensatory impulse to negate such feelings with violent misogynistic force. In return, she acts out her family history in front of him – we see him watching her bath another whore, then kiss her under his troubled gaze, in a way that seems to disempower rather than excite him. As he says with feigned bravado to Joanie in their final conversation, 'My lines are women, liquor, and rigged games of chance. Are you playing?'; but his trade, its objects of commerce are shaded differently from the 'fuck holes' that Swearengen or Mr Lee might provide. The *Bella Union* is premised on offering a more cultivated brand of woman for sale; as we see in his conversations, Tolliver has discovered a way of talking to women that acknowledges their subjectivity in order to 'take advantage of them in more elaborate and profitable ways'. But this also brings him closer to the complications of their exploitation, something that risks the stain of guilt: according to Milch, 'maybe the thing that shames him is the modernity of his understanding'.

In this way, Tolliver offers the clearest case of the fundamental doubleness which afflicts most of *Deadwood*'s characters, the various ways in which they 'spin against the way they drive'.[89] We only need glance at the elaborate nature of his almost dandified attire to take the hint that tough guy Tolliver has been feminised because his regular intimate dealings are with the women he exploits (his male confidants – Con and Leon – hardly offer him the strategic sounding board provided by the intellect of Adams, Bullock and even Farnum which Al has access to). In his discussions with the other writers, Milch folds this quality into the general interest of the show in the improvisation of society through the adaptation of habits of psychological pathology:

> If the best way to manoeuvre Stubbs is to use the locutions of solicitude, and that becomes automatic, suddenly Tolliver's found the thing had grown

132

in him and he's in love with her. Now the question is, can you adapt? Can you learn to love your love? Is that how love developed?

It is Tolliver's access to – however manipulative, exploitative and self-serving – the subjectivity of women that instils in him a modern sense of that subjectivity, so much so that Milch is able to claim in his book about the show that Tolliver would become, 'over the course of five seasons, the great philanthropist and feminist of Deadwood'.[90] For Milch, prostitution is a 'fundamental violation of the family unit … [where] the pimp's job is to continue to persuade the prostitute that she is a child who is dependent on him'. For Tolliver though, his moments of greatest vulnerability, hence violent misogyny, come when those roles threaten to reverse. Most vividly we see this happening with the arrival of Joanie's older business partner Maddie at the beginning of the second season; faced with the prospect of her leaving, his cruel, bitter fury is hardly suppressed beneath a veneer of childish glee: 'All take the air while Maddie hears the happy news? Let's go get the fucking crone. I feel like a boy. I feel like skipping.' Outside on his balcony he lines up his whores and pours liquor into their open 'yaps' in 'celebration' – in fact of course a display of his power, further augmented by offering as his 'gift' to them, Doris, a young blonde whore, telling her to pack the 'rags you been wiping the come off with'. As Joanie leaves, he turns away holding onto the balcony and enters a reverie of vicious misogyny:

133

> TOLLIVER: Don't fucking talk to me like I'm a monkey. Get those cunts out of here. Don't believe there's no good women till you seen one with maggots in her eyes.   ('A Lie Agreed Upon, Part I')

What Tolliver sees in Joanie's eyes is pity for him and it reduces him to an infant, something less than a man; ultimately his contempt for the childlike in himself expresses what we cannot know but surely suspect as a terrible relation with the woman who dominated him as a child, validating in his case what Farnum, in a moment of teaching his 'pet'

Richardson, describes as mother love or really a 'murderous hatred and a desire for revenge'.

As a professional whose income depends on playing the gambling percentages, it is significant that his failures are missteps characterised by Wolcott, at the moment Tolliver tries to extort him for his sexual twistedness, as 'overplay[ing] his hand'. He does this by typically misjudging the extent to which what has to be made *explicit* in order to be understood and acted on must also in part remain *implicit* and unsaid in the social world in order for it to have any force or grip at all. His calling together of the 'town elders' to rebuke Utter for his beating of Wolcott in the street in revenge for killing the whores leaves him tipping his hat as to his involvement in its cover-up and his collusion with the Hearst interests; his clumsy attempt to extort Hearst by reveal-ing to the press Wolcott's murderous sex crimes, are done with an absurd theatrical turn involving him pretending to dialogue with God, which only stiffens Hearst's resolve to break him. He seems destined to forego those alliances based on friendship and goodwill and to act as a subordinate to the larger forces he cannot help resenting for their emasculating nature; he welcomes their patronage but has to suffer the childlike or doglike subordination to them and their laconic agents, Wolcott, Lee and finally the sinister and mostly silent Mr Newman.

It is an index of Tolliver's malevolence that, while Al's subordinates gradually develop their individual voices – even Jewel offers some smart backchat – Cy's involvement with his seem destined for blood or worse. Trixie leaves Al for Star, but eventually they get along like old lovers, sharing a past; when Joanie leaves Cy he takes up with a younger whore, Lila (Meghan Glennon) who we see by the third season is ruined by heroin addiction; her replacement, an even younger whore called Janine (Sarah Pachelli), is ritually humiliated and mocked by Tolliver, who renames her 'Stupid'.

But if Tolliver's failure to cultivate a 'flock' marks him out as different in capacity from Al, how to assess Joanie in contrast to the socially adept and romantically settled Trixie? The idea of her seeking independence – 'taking wing from the nest' – is a motif established early on in the first season when she attends Hickok's funeral on her own and later wanders through the muddy thoroughfare looking for a place to set up the brothel Cy has promised to back. Kim Dickens plays this wonderfully as an adult appearing lost and childlike in a grown-up world, fearful yet defiantly kind as she converses with Charlie Utter about whether his new town clothes look appropriate. Utter is clearly in love with her and his role as her confidante-cum-therapist reinforces the welcoming oddness of this improvised community. Her friendship with Maddie initially appears likewise to be one of tutelage and education: 'The only guaranteed outcome, Honey, is contracting to get fucked …', she tells her, 'They get led by their dicks. Our cunts lead us we lose our only edge.' But catastrophically for Joanie, Maddie's selfish ambition to exploit Wolcott's intentions toward the whore she 'has on ice', Carrie (Izabella Miko), brings Joanie's ambition for independence to a murderous conclusion. After Joanie has a private session with an uninterested Wolcott, he later muses to Carrie:

> WOLCOTT: I sense Miss Stubbs has fucked a relative.
> CARRIE: It's a big club. ('Requiem for a Gleet')

For Carrie that means, perhaps, that both she and Wolcott belong to that club as well; the latter offers to sublimate such destructive behaviour in a perspective stretching back to the Greeks, when he offers to regale the *Chez Amis* women with stories of 'gods fornicating with mortals, the endless incest, fathers upon daughters upon sisters'. This reference locates Joanie's abuse in an epic tradition. Maddie's failure to prepare Joanie for the monstrous nature of Wolcott leaves her to rationalise him herself. For his part, Wolcott seems genuinely puzzled by his murderous behaviour. After Cy has cleaned up evidence of Wolcott's murders, Joanie awaits her fate in the empty *Chez Amis*. When she witnesses Wolcott's momentary indecision when he returns, she uses the opportunity to exercise her own unpractised independent voice. Smashing a bottle across his head she cries: 'You leave me alone! I got a fucking gun … get the fuck out … lock the front fucking door!'

Wolcott and Carrie

This seems to be the first time she's ever shouted at a man; it is all he needs to put him in his place. Chastened, he is even polite to Jane, who has belatedly come to guard Joanie, as he walks bleeding from the brothel.

In the finale of the second season we see Jane and Joanie together, dressed up for Alma and Ellsworth's wedding; all such malevolence seems, as it did at the end of the first, put in its place. The celebratory intensity of the wedding party, vouchsafed by Alma's 'Eleanor Roosevelt' voiceover where she seems to sacrifice the full experience of sensual agency in a life that seems to be 'living me ... not a moment of it ... my own', for the public service of staying in the camp with the family which has accrued around her. For blood and kinship ties seem to breed nothing but abuse and abandonment which, along with other stimuli absorbed in childhood, become manifest in pathological forms of acting out in adulthood. Instead the 'families' we see thrive in *Deadwood* form up through habit, effort and reaching out between unrelated individuals.[91] Alma's decision to stay and marry seems to unify the camp; the music that accompanies her wedding celebrations expressively underscores this.

In these final scenes, as the sounds and music of the wedding unify the camp, Al Swearengen is supreme. He cunningly outmanoeuvres Hearst the mining magnate – whose shadow of power is cast across this season before he even arrives, and yet who appears genial and unthreatening when he does – to allow Wu to defeat the evil Mr Lee, aided in the spirit of pantomime by Adams, Dority and Burns dressed in Oriental-style masks and costumes. Cochran teaches restorative breathing exercises to Mose Manuel; as he raises and lowers his arms a rack focus reveals the violent drop of Wolcott's suicide by hanging in the barn behind him.[92] His body swings from the noose as if dangling from the spinning bottom of the earth. The music continues, an emblem of the unifying potential of art; it even infects the skip-step of Cochran and Swearengen's tapping fingers on his balcony. Below him, Wu cuts off his ponytail (queue) in a gesture of solidarity and belonging, saying, 'Wu, America!' 'That'll hold you tight to her tit', replies Swearengen, holding his own as if *he* is at this moment America itself (we can glimpse here something of what lies beneath the seemingly audacious claim in the transcripts that Swearengen might have been President). The world is dancing to Swearengen's tune, and even the recalcitrant Bullock, after acting as witness to the treaty that absorbs Deadwood into Dakota county, decides to go home (Al directs him, 'To your fucking right'). He is a kind of director, having 'narrated' a view of the camp to Merrick earlier in the season before his illness, and arranged the treaty with Commissioner Jarry on the premise of the most absurd fiction about a county politician commissioner making backroom deals with a bag over his head. As he watches *his* Deadwood from the balcony he is even accompanied by a character he has confected: 'The Chief' a disembodied head in a wooden box, a pure theatrical prop he uses to provide his soliloquies with an interlocutor. Al is at the height of his powers and *Deadwood* at this point seems complete as an organic series: cancellation would have meant we had a tragically short but satisfyingly whole work.

The beginning of the third season, set a mere six weeks after the second, offers a radical shift of register. It opens with a beautiful yet

137

ominous long shot of dawn over the camp, the black shape of a lone bird overhead, with the camera moving down through rosy clouds to the grey mud of the main street, light turning to dark. Al steps into frame in extreme close-up, enacting through his movement a rack-focus composition; 'Fixing toward a bloody outcome boss', Dan calls from the street below, and the first action is the apparently racist killing of a Cornish miner in the *Gem*, although it transpires that Hearst has set up the killing in order to stake his claim to do what he wants in Al's territory. This first episode continues by emphatically and efficiently restating the happy settlement of season two's conclusion only to systematically unpick that organic unity. This is most clearly seen in the way the early composition of shots incorporates groups of characters with backgrounds busy with the flow of commerce while, by the end of the episode, we see characters isolated in empty, static shots. Thematically, lightness becomes dark too: we have the mild comedy of grown men nervous about public speaking – Star, Utter, Bullock and Nuttall's barman Harry Manning (Brent Sexton) are all standing for election, and the hustings, we discover, will take place that night (Harry, Tom along with Steve (Michael Harney) and the shit-stirrer Rutherford (Ted Mann) make up another family of tertiary characters who 'live' in the *No. 10 Saloon*). There is also Alma fussily directing Ellsworth in arranging the furniture in her new house; we see established domestic regularities – Sofia taking Martha's hand on the way to the *Chez Amis*, now the location of Deadwood's schoolhouse, to 'bake bread again'; Swearengen continues in his role of the town's 'show-runner', this time organising 'sets' and the movement of his 'actors' by getting Star to buy a house where an adjoining hole has been cut into Shaughnessy's flophouse next door, allowing Trixie to enter the next Mayor's rooms out of sight of a potentially disdainful public view, although, given the nature of Deadwood's public, one suspects the real reason is Al's love of stage-setting.

We see a recovered Mose Manuel happily taking up his role as a 'watchman' outside the *Chez Amis*, which has been transformed into the schoolhouse, and bickering with Jane, who observes Joanie walking

toward the *Bella Union* 'like a moth to a flame'. This last movement
alerts us to a regressive shift; when Cramed stabs Tolliver at the
wedding, Joanie does not rush to help but withholds herself, staying
alongside Utter and Jane, and telling another *Bella Union* girl to 'see to
him honey'. Now she has returned to what is clearly Tolliver's declining
empire, as he lays in bed, gripping a Bible in the pretence of having
found God; Leon and Con's bickering has a brittle edge, and ominously
the whores are in disarray with Lila 'on the needle' and their backroom
smelling 'like a hogwhore's cunt'. As Joanie tries to whip the whores
into shape we see again her ability to act as business partner to Cy;
the work animates her, gives her a purpose, an authority but in the
corrupted history of her family it is that of an unnatural mother and
daughter. Earlier we had witnessed her readying for suicide in her dark
room at Shaughnessy's flophouse:

> TOLLIVER: You listen to me young lady, what brings a gun to the temple is
> lack of gainful occupation and being useful to others. I don't see you trying
> to kill yourself here. All you do here is good for the girls and me too.
> JOANIE: I don't want to run girls no more.
> TOLLIVER: That's turning from your gift and your training.
> JOANIE: When you speak I feel like it's the devil talking.
>
> ('Tell Your God to Ready for Blood')

139

Of all *Deadwood*'s women, Joanie is the one who suffers the most
spiritual desolation, unrelieved by the temporary solaces of booze (Jane)
or drugs (Alma) and her meetings with the kind, grizzled Charlie Utter
take on a tone of self-loathing desperation. 'If I could I'd tear my skin off.
If I could I'd tear out my eyes', she tells him. As Emerson acknowledges,
suffering does not bring with it the consolation of insight or access to
truth; even at its worst it can feel false. Later she breaks down in his post
office-cum-jailhouse, telling Charlie about her wish to see the children
walking into the *Chez Amis* schoolhouse: 'I wish once I could care for
those little ones. Just once instead of doing what I did.' Nested in this
poignant plea to negate the terrible weight of the past, is the apprehension

of her desire to nurture rather than corrupt as she did as a child with her sisters. This accounts, in part, for her involvement with Jane. In the latter episodes of the second season we see her bath and dress Jane, preparing her for the wedding, effectively mothering her out of her alcoholism.

Like Cochran, whose bellicosity she shares, Jane is a vivid individuality, but unlike the other women she never settles in the camp, until – perhaps (we will never know), the final episode when Joanie wraps her in Hickok's bearskin. She leaves camp before the first season ends and returns in the second 'to die' as she tells the Doc. Her loud obscenities and bravado mask a shy, childish fear, and her persistent drunkenness seems to be a means of stilling her unmanly capacity for warm-hearted care that we witness as an audience as she talks softly to the recovering Sofia. Robin Weigert, herself noticeably shy in interviews, describes Jane's 'extraordinary generosity of spirit … being too sensitive for the life [she's] led' in relation to David Milch's behaviour:

> David's physical behaviour is a gold mine. Particularly where Jane's in a position of being kind of caught out, a little self conscious or something like that … . There is a showmanship and there's a surprising shyness at the same time … . When you see David with his children or his dogs, you see his heart bursts wide open in the presence of these loved creatures. I think it's the same with this character. She cannot help it, her heart just falls open. [93]

This signals the spiritual sensitivity of large hearts overwhelmed at the prospect of the magnitude of their response to the world, something covered or suppressed with obscenity and drugs. Jane's friendships also seem pre-adult – the bickering with Utter reaches a pitch when she refuses his offer of a job in his freight business ('drink mare's piss'); her drinking with 'Nigger General' Fields and Aunt Lou (Cleo King) demonstrates the drunkard's desire to cultivate a community of drinkers as much as it signals her friendly nature. Her meeting with Joanie at the end of the first episode of the third season takes place in the empty *Chez Amis*: the camp is now in 'disarray'. Al, threatened by Hearst, cancels the election speeches, Jane has fallen asleep and pissed herself; Joanie, isolated in the frame, asks that Jane remain asleep inside: 'Every day,' says the latter, 'takes figuring out all over again how to fucking live.'

Jane and Joanie are one of only two pairs of characters we see fall in love during the show. Alma and Seth's torrid attraction is clearly pathological for both of them, and Star and Trixie get together early in the show before we have sufficient sense of either to calibrate the significance of them coming together. Jane's request as Joanie bathes her to 'sponge my fucking tits if that's what you do' carries the gauche awkwardness of the ingénue novice, a request masked in her typical way as crude assertion. Listen to the tender way Joanie cares for her:

> JOANIE: It's nothing like that Jane.
> JANE: Well, what's it like then. I never had a sister.
> JOANIE: I had two. And I slept with both of them. I don't know why God let me or if he forgives me when I pray, but I'd never hurt you Jane or touch you if you didn't want.
> JANE: I believe that. But I don't want to open my eyes. But you can go ahead and kiss me if that's what you fucking do.   ('Unauthorized Cinnamon')

What *Deadwood* is good at – *unmatched* in any form or media – is its mixing of associations, probing for the feeling that moves the characters, the scene, us, without making them hostage to an insistence on clear meaning. The glow that brings out the haze. More than any other character, Jane is emblematic of this achievement: we cleave to the secret worth of her dirty, beautiful personhood. In this scene, when the two of them kiss – the water, the closed eyes, Jane's childlike wonder at her luck, Joanie's practised care (we have seen her bathing other women) open us up in unexplored ways to shadings and gradations of sense and feeling that we yearn to explain even as we welcome their presence. We feel growth here.

That growth is bound up with teaching. In a show blessed with fine characters depicted by deeply committed actors, it is easy but wrong to neglect Anna Gunn's patient, steadfast and sensible

141

rendering of Martha Bullock, who finds herself a role as the camp's educator. Arguably the camp is constituted by the momentum and forces released after the slaughter of the Metz family leaves Sofia alone in need of protection; Martha also loses her child in order to become properly part of the camp, her grief vividly struck across her bright face when she rushes inside to weep over her son's open coffin at his funeral. And yet she lives, finding herself closer to Bullock, salving his previous maniacal awkwardness in the domestic setting which always seemed to confine him. Television series allow us to experience the 'after' of such terrible events, and witness the upbuilding of life as it continues (for example, we get a tender scene in their bed at the end of the day, where she patiently listens to Bullock's tedious complaints about his role in the conflict resolution between Steve/Hostetler dispute).

Martha's teaching shows her unencumbered by defects of the spirit, but acutely aware of the impact of her work.[94] We hear her read to the class from Charles Northend's 1851 textbook, *Dictation Exercises*, including the line 'Indians are sometimes very cruel.'[95] It would be wrong (in fact it is a classic *Deadwood* misdirect) to take Martha's hesitation at this line as a modern revulsion at the way racism was woven into the fabric of education. It is of course important that we, in the present, experience it as precisely that, but the hesitation is in the service of demonstrating how rote learning – habit and repetition of any kind – freezes people in the past; it confines our understanding in ways we experience as outdated and regressive. This is Martha's discovery, and the reason for the hesitation is her realisation that teaching needs to bring things alive for its pupils. Martha's request that Jane relate to the schoolchildren her stories of scouting for Custer heralds a process by which these women, with Charlie and Mose, begin to constitute themselves as a grouping around the schoolchildren; her spontaneity in mocking the 'puffed-up' Armstrong Custer also delights the children, bringing history alive in front of them – a history very much bound up with cruelty – in ways the textbook only deadens. Jane takes on the role as a 'behind-the-scenes' voice of authentic Western

Jane teaching the class

history, supplying fascinating details of its *mise en scène* – such as Custer's vanity, voice and habits – that only a witness could know. Growth happens here too; Jane quits drinking for the day and bathes before she enjoys her moment in front of the class.

When Hearst's vicious glowering grip over the camp is reaching its peak with the infiltration of armed mercenaries, Martha and Bullock walk a line of children through the main thoroughfare toward the new school; the line is led by Joanie and Jane, the latter sick with booze, holding on to the former. The new school was built around a tree which remains growing in its centre and Joanie, in another conversation with her friend Charlie, laments the fact that she did not discover who the man was who built it around the tree or why he did it:

> CHARLIE: Why does she need to know where the man got to for Mrs Bullock
> to tell the children about the tree?
> JOANIE: To finish the story.
> CHARLIE: More than where the man got to once he was through, I'd think
> the story was of the tree and the schoolhouse built around it. I guess you're
> right though. I guess children are like that, wanting to know all the

Joanie's healing participation in the everyday: 'I was just stopping by to say good morning.'

information. I guess that's how they are. You got something to send Miss Stubbs?

JOANIE: I was just stopping by to say good morning.   ('Amateur Night')

The school is a place where childhood should be protected, as well as the place where we learn to leave childhood behind by accepting we cannot always get the whole picture, the finished story. When Cy attempts to breach its perimeter his contempt for this is vivid ('Is that a darling fucking treehouse in the precious fucking branches for the shitheel little kids to play amongst in jolly joy?'), and it takes the nervous team of Joanie, Jane and Mose to ward him off. In a mood of forgiveness and gratitude Joanie even returns to the *Bella Union* afterwards to thank him for keeping her alive long enough to experience the love she has with Jane. Hearing her voice makes him ache for her and in the negation of that feeling he responds with the line that forms the epigraph to this chapter.

The rack-focus gesture constantly reminds us that we fail if we try to locate the meaning of life exclusively in one – say, our own – experience: there is more going on around us that may bear upon things and not all of it will be clearly defined. When a drunk disturbs Al's sleep with a loud solitary lament for his bad luck, and is next morning discovered in the mud outside the *Gem* with a broken neck, Burns, Dority and Al wonder if Hearst was behind it, leaving a message for them. The fact that things *just happen* is one of the harder lessons for grown-up humans to learn since part of our very hardwiring makes us crave meaning and we tend to draw on the habits and patterns of the past to fill the chasms of meaning and understanding that regularly confront us. Equally, *Deadwood* reminds us that what is 'behind people' – their impulses and desires – forms a context whereby each strives to cope with the pressure of the sediments of the past while seeking, each new morning, if they can see clearly enough, to renew themselves through the habits of sociality and our testimony and debt to one another in the present. Hence, *Deadwood* is not really about an *absence* – of law, or society or civilisation – but about the continued entangling *presence* of the past, and our efforts in the here and now to live it.

8 Communication and Civilisation

The great thing is to last and get your work done and see and hear and learn and understand; and write when there is something that you know; and not before; and not too damned much after. Let those who want to save the world if you can get to see it clear and as a whole. Then any part you make will represent the whole if it's made truly. The thing to do is work and learn to make it.

Ernest Hemingway, Death in the Afternoon

DORITY: If we know Hearst is coming, boss, why the fuck don't we strike first?
AL: From the moment we leave the forest, Dan, it's all a giving up and adjusting.

'I Am Not the Fine Man You Take Me For'

Like Clell Watson, David Milch uses speech to animate his worlds. The short film on the season three DVD of *Deadwood* called 'Respecting the Process' shows him speaking the lines aloud, and revising them in detail, as they are typed by an amanuensis onto a large computer screen in front of him. This is writing as speaking, a very public form of testimony to one's art, but the film only allows us to glimpse this method of 'channelling' the voices of the characters. The transcripts of writing meetings that took place before, during and after shooting throughout each year the show was in production, are dominated by Milch's vivid and dense articulation of the dramatic trajectory, the motivations, the psychology, history and culture of the characters as well as discourses on art, politics, religion, literature and history, confirming Blake Bailey's assertion that Milch is 'the most spontaneously articulate human being I have ever encountered'.[96] The spoken word becomes the written word becomes the spoken word in the mouths of the characters: the alchemy of dramatic fiction is in this mysterious journey of energy from one voice to another, voices which set the world around them in motion.

Deadwood's writing is an emphatically collaborative achievement and its organisation was otherwise conventional for multistrand long-form dramatic television fiction. A regular team of writers worked with Milch contributing to the development of the stories; scenes and episodes would be divided between them and subsequently evaluated, discussed and revised. Milch would always do the final revision, however, although the extent of the changes he made would vary. Some of his regulars like Ted Mann, who is officially credited with the most writing credits on the show (and whose scripts were revised the least), had worked with Milch before on other shows such as *NYPD Blue*. Regina Corrado, Elizabeth Sarnoff, Jody Worth also wrote multiple episodes. The writers' room was also clearly a teaching room with writing interns and upcoming staff writers as well as actors doing their part (two of the latter, Ricky Jay and W. Earl Brown are credited with their own episodes); Gregg Fienberg, the main producer, was a patient and caring presence too, as well as directing an episode himself. To talk about *Deadwood*'s creative achievement only in terms of 'Milch's art' would be like talking about the town itself only in terms of Swearengen's actions and ambition: it covers a lot that is important, but misses a hell of a lot that is crucial too. Nonetheless, my account of *Deadwood*'s achievement necessarily privileges Milch because as show runner his authorship comes down to a question of ultimate artistic *authority*, and in this show it is hard to see much that escaped his attention or approval. Crucially, he was around on set for the actors providing encyclopaedic backstory as well as direction that went beyond the meaning of the words. As Anna Gunn says about his involvement,

147

I know people have said the Shakespeare thing but it's true – I find the
language leads you where you need to go and then when David comes onto
the set what I find often is that you've got all these beautiful words there
and then he'll say, 'Why don't you just try this gesture? Why don't you just
try putting that down over there,' and it could be seemingly the most minor
thing but … it will illuminate the entire scene for me.[97]

Acts of writing and communication are central to *Deadwood*
from its early shots of Bullock writing in his journal, to the flurry
of telegrams intercepted and exchanged that become crucial to
Swearengen's intelligence warfare with Hearst in the final season. The
camp itself is littered with writing, and nearly every shot has some
evidence of the written word, either in shop signs and advertising
banners, or menus and prices – words and symbols are part of the visual
texture of the place. We also see many of the characters writing – letters,
treaties or contracts or in the case of Wu and, later Hearst, pictures
and pictographs in need of interpretation. Being 'lettered' is a key
evolutionary advantage in the camp and the exchange of information
is central to the shifting ecology of the town's mood.

We have already seen how the muscular power of Al's speech
creates action, but his oratorical gift is also the source of his ability as a
teacher, who seeks out responsive students of human nature like himself.
This is in contrast to others, like Hearst who merely abuses his
employees ('show me you're lettered and worthy of my employ!', he
barks at his doomed henchman Barrett (Jared Snyder)), or Tolliver whose
pedagogy also leaves a lot to be desired ('your initiative and leadership
abilities and stick-fuckin-to-it-tiveness are all in fucking question', he
says to the bewildered Con and Leon). Al adopts Silas Adams as his most
promising student and heir apparent; Titus Welliver plays him with quiet,
dedicated, intelligent charm. The naive comedy of his shyness is exploited
in the episodes where he is entrapped (Milch's word for it is 'cuntstruck')
by the Pinkerton posing as a tutor, Miss Isringhausen. Equally, his
political acuity means he is an important intermediary for Al in
negotiations with Hearst and Tolliver. Like Al he has an aptitude as

148

Al as teacher and his students ...

Trixie and Adams ...

Blazanov and Merrick

reader of moods, signs and codes. (There are other versions of growthful teacher–student relationships in the show, such as Cochran/Jane and Aunt Lou/Richardson.)

The major communicative force in the camp is Merrick's newspaper, and he too becomes Al's student. The connecting door between the *Gem* and the *Deadwood Pioneer* is a conduit through which Al, Merrick and eventually the telegraph operator Blazanov, communicate and exchange information. Merrick's interest in information is, in part, fuelled by a curiosity for gossip, and Al is good at deflating the former's claims of fealty to abstract ideals. After Hearst has sent men over to commit murder on Al's territory in the *Gem*, killing a Cornishman, Merrick demands to know what the gunfire he heard meant. Al refuses to tell him:

> MERRICK: Are we at war now here in the camp? Has that fact been suppressed as well? Absent formal declaration, Al, information which affects this community is not my prerogative to disseminate: to do so is my sacred duty.
>
> AL: Whores currently disseminating a dose for example?
>
> MERRICK: To inform within decency's limits. We've had this discussion before.
>
> AL: Citizens better die postulating that touch indecent ink.
>
> MERRICK: Make a list of the infected whores and account for this morning's gunfire and I'll publish it all.
>
> AL: I won't, fucking Merrick, because neither's to my fucking interests, just as you owning a printing press proves only that you've an interest in the truth, meaning up to a fucking point – slightly more than the rest of us maybe, but short of a fucking anointing or the shouldering of a sacred burden, unless of course the print press was a gift of an angel.
>
> ('I Am Not the Fine Man You Take Me For')

After his press is smashed by Con and Leon at Tolliver's instructions, for refusing to publish Commissioner Jarry's announcement casting doubt on the validity of the gold claims, Al discovers Merrick slumped in his office, passive and inert, in the slough of despond. In *Deadwood*, alone and passive means close to death, the suspension of the human. Al brings him back into the world with a slap across the face and a lesson, that echoes William James's famous description of the 'heroic man' who can '*stand* this Universe': 'Pain or damage don't end the world, or despair, of fucking beatings. The world ends when you're dead. Until then, you've got more punishment in store. Stand it like a man. And give some back.'[98]

Al's interest in Merrick's work, evident in the first season when he supervises the text of the plague announcement, seems to point to an alternative career for him. As he says to Dan while reading with some pride, the special 'plague' issue of the *Pioneer* he helped author, 'Different path taken at certain forks in the road, who knows what kind of fucking joint we'd be in now.' I take this to mean that Al's alternative career would be not as a writer or director of events, but as an editor, the behind-the-scenes power in the mould of Cary Grant's hard-boiled Walter Burns from *His Girl Friday* (1940). We get that sense of a busy city paper editor able to process dense volleys of current events when Al is restored to his office seat after his illness in 'E. B. Was Left Out'. With the camera behind him, he pivots in his office chair, firing off instructions and responding to events – interpreting the spectacle of Utter beating Wolcott in the street, appraising the significance of Tolliver's visit – with prescient expertise. And like an editor admonishing a trainee, he rebukes Merrick for penning an article designed to convince Yankton that Montana is courting Deadwood for annexation (Tolliver immediately grasps its crudity: 'Swearengen's put the paper man's boat to sea with a hold full of fucking bullshit'). Swearengen's criticism indicates his sensitivity to the detail of language; he uses a culinary trope to indicate that the scale of its lie negated the deception's dissembling grip: 'the truth, if only a pinch, must season every falsehood else the palate rebels,' he says; it needs, 'scale, amount, proportion'.

151

These public communications designed to deceive contrast with the private vocalisations that are closely anchored to the inner experience of their owners. The image of Milch speaking the characters' words aloud in a room is mirrored by the show's brilliant soliloquies and monologues. Farnum and Swearengen are the primary users, although others partake less regularly. These moments of auto-vocalisation typically deploy a silent or near-silent interlocutor – Richardson or Dolly (or, more exotically, the muddy puddle Leon discourses with) who, far from being an inert presence, contextualise the speech we hear. So we feel Richardson's uncomprehending victimhood in the face of Farnum's increasingly mad complaints and Dolly's exploitation as she fellates the drunken Al. And yet these figures do not negate the drama of what we hear which can be poignant itself, especially in Al's recounting of his abusive childhood and the moment of abandonment at the orphanage by his mother. Equally, we get to explore Al's thinking unencumbered by a necessity to explain to less quick-thinking underlings, in his 'conversations' with The Chief, the Indian head in a box he keeps in his office – the head that he had paid fifty dollars in bounty for, as a ruse to keep those drinking in the *Gem* after the Metz massacre. For all Al's work in moving the camp toward a civilised state of order, The Chief – however comically and ironically deployed – is a constant reminder that what counts as 'civilised' may depend on the violent exclusion and genocidal destruction of others.

If Deadwood is a 'second chance' for those who go there to make their way, the national scar that haunts any American fiction, not least one set in the Reconstruction era, is the fact of slavery. As we have seen the enslavement and instrumental usage of women is continuously prominent in the narrative and *mise en scène*. Indians, with the exception of the warrior who attacks Bullock, are a structuring absence. Structuring because we know that Deadwood 'being on Indian land' itself is stolen, and that the ethnic cleansing of the region is couched in the very instruments – treaties, laws – we witness again and again in the narrative as hostage to every kind of mendacity and avarice. What is left of the Sioux continues to be robbed by the state administrators charged with interacting with the Native American tribes even in their exclusion; as Silas Adams remarks to Commissioner Jarry, their siphoning off of Government assistance was 'regular as milking

Bessie … if it was less than ninety cents [on the dollar] you fucked generations of Indian agents to come'.[99]

Nevertheless *Deadwood*'s direct depiction of the nature of racism attempts to show that its repugnant currents of hatred are inhospitable to the growth and flourishing of the camp. Steve Fields, played selflessly by *NYPD Blue* veteran Michael Harney, emerges in the second season as a loudmouth spokesman for the prospectors violently unsettled by the notice Jarry has made Merrick release to the public in order to create doubt about the legitimacy of the gold claims. Steve plans to abduct the 'Nigger General' Samuel Fields in order to distract Bullock long enough to get at the Commissioner, who has been locked up for his own protection. Faced with a minor setback, his scheme becomes simply, 'just grab the nigger'. Franklyn Ajaye is equal to Harney's selflessness in his version of a real figure who described himself in the telephone book (Deadwood was one of the first places to be equipped with telephone lines) as a 'cosmopolite'. His character is well aware of the mortal danger whereby racism, attaching to a free-floating personal sense of grievance and resentment, allows its possessor to fantasise a moral system which in turn justifies any extent of violence: 'You stole my look at riches, you and your monkey cousins!', shouts Steve, as he spreads boiling pitch on the Nigger General's body.

It is the same knowledge of irrational retribution that makes Hostetler and the Nigger General flee the camp when the horse they were trying to castrate fatally tramples William Bullock. The guilt they feel about the harm done to Bullock's child (they do not yet realise he has died) gets bound up with Hostetler's sad resolution to destroy himself before he will again suffer the ignominy of being judged by white society. While the Nigger General embodies the agile mind trying to make its way through wit and cunning (we learn he was previously employed running messages from rich 'pot-gut shitheads to those fat-ass women they keep on the side'), Hostetler's admirable but deadly pride, his resistance to being judged by the whites, marks him as stricken with shame in what he views as his own complicity in his oppression, his outrage 'because he hates having Tommed his whole life'. As with Joanie

153

Stubbs, we see a figure who is hostage in the present to the continued wounding of the past.

The conflict between Steve, Hostetler and the Nigger General becomes an emblem of the wider limits of the camp's ability to provide a civilised settlement. The Nigger General, like Jane, who he befriends, has no fixed home, is a wanderer. Hostetler on the other hand has made a life and settled with property, selling Bullock the land that he builds his house on. When Hostetler catches Steve masturbating over the leg of Bullock's horse in his Livery he ties him up and threatens to kill him; the Nigger General negotiates Steve's release by having him sign a confession scratched on a chalk board: 'I fucked Bullock's horse.' When they return to camp to find Steve has been tending the Livery in their absence, Bullock, accepting Hostetler's spoken regret, arranges with them to transfer the property to Steve, an admission that the two of them cannot thrive together in the same place. But even this fails when, the transaction completed – each simultaneously signing the papers in a contrived synchronised ceremony – Steve requests that Hostetler return the chalk board. When they eventually find it hidden in the Livery, the writing has vanished, worn off by time; Steve will not accept it as 'the actual board' and Hostetler responds, 'I will not be called a fucking liar. I did *not* live my life for that.' He goes outside and shoots himself in the head with a rifle. This in turn prompts a frustrated, enraged Bullock, seeing his efforts end so tragically, to barge into the *Bella Union*, arrest and drag Hearst by the ear to jail, substantially raising the stakes of the conflict between him and the rest of the town. There is no relation between the two events, except that both Hearst and Steve represent implacable forces which refuse compromise. It is typical of *Deadwood* that it disdains in this storyline a 'Norman Lear' kind of reconciliation between the races and instead concentrates on the egregious effects of the immediacy of impulsive feeling – pride, resentment, suspicion and rage.

What are we to make of the fact that after all this trouble, the Nigger General ends up caring for Steve, who initially offers him partnership of the Livery (the alert viewer might note the signage Steve, discusses would read 'Fields & Fields Livery'), before being made an

Steve, Hostetler

imbecile by a horse kick to the skull? *Deadwood* does not decant into any simple allegorical meanings that stick in such cases as this; its depiction of settlement does not itself settle, but troubles, disturbs, seeks to push further amid dense webs of association whose strands cross and recross, meeting with the past and the future in strange scenes whose significance and importance we intuit or feel but cannot define or name with clarity.

Despite his belief in the power of gold to transcend all human division, Hearst is thoroughly implicated in this racism. His 'nigger cook', Aunt Lou Marchbanks is one of the many new elements arriving in town in the third episode of the third season. Hearst seems initially infantilised and delighted by her arrival, but when he discovers her son Odell (Omar Gooding) in her kitchen, he is clearly outraged that the comforts of his mother–child relationship with a servant has been disrupted. In a further turn that reinforces our sense of blood ties gone awry, we discover that Aunt Lou sent Odell to Liberia as a boy in order to protect him; we learn from him that there 'American niggers steal off the African, till the English cheat us out of it'. Her decision has created his seething resentment and desire for revenge; Odell has returned like a black Ahab to somehow harpoon Hearst with his story of a gold find in Africa. For Aunt Lou, this represents the very thing she wanted to avoid for her son, a desire to immerse himself in the destructive racist thicket of American history:

> AUNT LOU: I sent you so that the hell that was coming here for niggers wouldn't burn you up.
> ODELL: There's plenty of fire in Liberia.
> AUNT LOU: I can't undo what I done Odell, any more than you can, searching out hurt.
> ODELL: I ain't searching no hurt out.
> AUNT LOU: We all get our portion. We don't need to draw it to us.
>
> ('Unauthorized Cinnamon')

'True Colors', the third episode of the final season, comes after an unusual two-week hiatus between Hearst symbolically castrating Swearengen by chopping off his finger at the end of 'I Am Not the Fine Man You Take Me For', and Al alone in his office, clearly paralysed by indecision. Hearst has clearly put Al 'off his feed' – he cannot sleep or achieve a hard-on despite Dolly's best efforts. He is restored only by Trixie's lively admonition (as audience surrogate) to keep fighting ('I can't imagine that cocksucker got to you. Or that you're folding your fucking tent. The last shot ain't yet fired'), and the arrival of several new

156

characters by stagecoach. Indeed, by the third season, there are so many stories that the viewer is encouraged to work like Swearengen in quickly synthesising the meaning of people and events in front of them. Central to these arrivals is an old friend of his, the theatrical impresario, Jack Langrishe. His troupe is a collection of two women, the Countess Berman (Julie Ariola), an older matriarchal figure with a Germanic accent, Claudia (Cynthia Ettinger), a buxom young actress, whose brittle relationship with Langrishe is a hole card we never see turned; they are later joined by Chesterton (Aubrey Morris), an elderly dying actor and Bellegarde (Dennis Christopher), his effeminate and fragile but slightly younger carer.[100]

These new characters rapidly take on a life of their own in the camp and begin to occupy more screen time, a fact acknowledged in the odd way regulars Al and Seth watch, as mere spectators, Aunt Lou running down the muddy thoroughfare past them ('Not quick, but she does seem full of purpose' – Al has no idea what is going on). Their presence expands our range of attention, thickening the delay of the ever-threatened clash between Swearengen's forces and Hearst's. They also inhabit some of the show's most brilliant scenes, for instance, the moment over dinner where Odell dines with Hearst, the latter casting doubts on Odell's identity as First Deacon of Monrovia. Hearst claims he is acting 'less with our Saviour's qualities of character than Adam's or someone pretending to his innocence'. 'Before he met the Serpent' is Odell's astute reply. The Biblical resonance here is brilliantly and comically offset by having the supposedly dim Richardson report to Aunt Lou, who is waiting nearby in the kitchen and anxious about her son's fate, that Odell is 'holding his fucking own'. Or there is the exquisite sequence played pitch perfectly by Brian Cox as Langrishe and Aubrey Morris as the dying Chesterton, where on the 'stage' in the *Chez Amis*, they enact the Gloucester–Edgar 'Dover' mock-suicide scene from *King Lear*. By internalising the methods and medium of dramatic fiction, the scene asks us to wonder at the relationship between the forms and patterns of art and the life it draws its energy and inspiration from. What are we to do then with Chesterton's claim that the masks depicting

Thalia and Melpomone are a 'big lie': 'Same damn thing Jack, comedy and tragedy'? His final words – 'Line ... line' – imply that his creators have withdrawn *their* breath, *their* speech. And yet I suspect that the influx of these new characters is what makes the third season difficult for those who want to cling to the familiar comforts and characters of the first two. While I recognise the discomfort of adjustment, for me the infusion of new voices installs new riches and opens deeper possibilities for the show's evolution. But it is a risk, as if a circus car full of clowns has arrived in camp with its strange and unpredictable cargo of new elements tumbling out. One of the key structural attractions of the first two seasons was that the friction and resolution, impasse and transcendence that the characters experience within scenes ripple out into the overall structure of each episode, so that scenes 'speak' to scenes, and episodes are in conversation and negotiation with one another. The first season was structured around the dialectical opposition of Bullock and Swearengen, which eventually becomes a synthesis of their interests; in the second, the dramatic opposition is between the town and the outside economic and political forces of Hearst (represented by Wolcott and Lee) and Yankton (represented by Commissioner Hugo Jarry). The third season makes another turn, with Hearst as the deeper, cosmic force, an individual, who absorbs the political and economic into himself (thanks to Stephen Tobolowsky's superb performance we get a vivid image as Jarry describes himself to Hearst as a 'newly hatched bird' seeking sustenance from his mouth). Season two has already instructed us as to the awesome power of Hearst's economic and political forces: now that he is installed within the camp, what can it muster in opposition to him?

Hearst is a figure of epic destruction and Biblical Evil, but the show is careful to also show him as an ordinary man hostage to everyday frustrations. The show implies that he has something missing in his character which makes him unable to inhabit the human places of solidarity. Hearst himself recognises this, saying to Odell, 'the necessities I'm prepared to accept make me outcast'. But when we first see him at the end of the second season he seems more like a genial professor, whose intolerance for Wolcott's murderous behaviour implies a different moral capacity, rejecting the latter's claim that the earth speaks to him 'saying there is no sin': 'It tells me where the colour is. That's all it tells me.' But we also get hints of the scale of Hearst's disruptive danger when, as the Garret–Ellsworth wedding ceremony is completed, we hear the sound of Hearst's sledgehammer destroying the walls of the *Grand Central Hotel* he has just bought from Farnum. Later he knocks a hole in the front of the hotel, forming an improvised veranda where he, across from Swearengen, surveys the camp.

This image of both men at opposite sides of the main thoroughfare reinforces the symbolic sense of them as different sides of the scale, with the central thoroughfare the medium where their forces clash. This is made explicit in the epic fight to the death between their respective giants, Dan Dority and Captain Turner (the latter described by the former as a 'sea creature'). The fight returns us to the imagery of the primordial and prehistoric as the two of them battle in the mud and puddles of *Deadwood*'s street, among the hanging carcasses and shabby torn and tattered onlookers. The spectacle recapitulates in an extended fashion the Swearengen–Bullock fight, but whereas that resulted in unblocking the energy of the camp, little seems resolved once Dority has plucked out Turner's eye and clubbed him to death. Indeed, without Turner as interlocutor for the playing out of plans and thoughts, Hearst is suddenly much more volatile and dangerous.

The season is dominated by the choice which faces Swearengen's side – ultimately the entire town (even Tolliver comes to the meeting of the camp elders to decide what to do about Hearst) – as to whether to wage war on Hearst, whose 'deeper pockets' and economic underpinning shield him from either direct or concealed attack. As Al tells Langrishe, who has been treating Hearst's bad back in a display of mystic quackery:

AL: If that cocksucker hadn't shareholders, you could murder him while you adjusted his back.

159

Al and Hearst on either side of the scales. In between, Dority and Captain Turner fight to the death

LANGRISHE: Serpent's teeth – shareholders. Ten thousand would rise to
replace him.

This trope colours Hearst's power with mythic and Biblical overtones,
specifically the sowing of dragon's teeth (a task given to Jason by King
Aeetes of Colchis) to grow an army of invincible warriors; but these are
also the *Serpent*'s teeth, so Hearst incorporates an Evil so fundamental
that it cannot be destroyed, only delayed or moved. When his
mercenaries (at one point Hearst calls them 'janissaries' in another
gesture toward more ancient conflicts) arrive in the town, Al says,
'Leviathan smiles' in a reference to Langrishe's suggestion that the 'best
connection to leviathan may not be by harpoon'. This reference to *Moby
Dick* reinforces the sense of Hearst's abstract otherness, even though his
naturalistic depiction is never undermined. His horsemen thunder up
and down the thoroughfare disrupting commerce, knocking Wu down
into the dirt; their black uniforms infect the visual field, so that the out-
of-focus background elements noticeably darken because of their
presence. It is important that one of the first acts of civil violence they
initiate is breaking the foot of a guest queuing up for breakfast at the
Grand Central: they intend to disrupt the habits and routines that
constitute what William James calls 'the flywheel of civilisation'. Later
the pistoleros pick a fight with historical guest stars Morgan (Austin
Nichols) and Wyatt Earp in the street, providing a hint of action in an
otherwise blocked dramatic situation.

161

Balanced against Hearst's contagion of the thoroughfare is the
escort of the schoolchildren as they walk down the same main street, led
by the lesbian couple Jane with Joanie, with Bullock and Martha taking
the rear. The script notes that Hearst observes them below, 'with brave,
private resignation, that by dint of his greatness, Life and Destiny have
denied him the simple joys of having to do with his fellow and their
pain-in-the-balls offspring'. This represents Swearengen's response to
Hearst's disorder, violence and chaos – civilisation, education and
growth against domination, authoritarian power and control. Most of
all what Hearst is lacking – and what also gives him the ability to look at

the vast mountainous outcrops of the earth's crust and see gold – is a sense of *scale*: as Al says to Bullock:

> Running his holdings like a despot, I grant, has a fucking logic. It's the way I fucking run mine. It's the way I'd run my home if I fucking had one. But there's no practical need for him to run the fucking camp. That's out of scale. It's out of proportion, and it's a warped unnatural impulse, this fucking cocksucker. ('Tell Your God to Ready for Blood')

He also lacks the facility for decent conversation without invoking his power. This is evident in the scenes where he stamps his authority over Bullock ('I put *you* on Notice'), Tolliver ('your duties will be to answer like a dog when I call') and Alma ('You are reckless Madam, you indulge yourself') who he 'nearly rapes', according to his own testimony. He's proud of his Indian name of 'the Boy the Earth Talks to' since, as he tells Aunt Lou, 'it's the only goddamn conversation I care to have'. Later, in one of the show's final scenes, Langrishe points to the essential childishness of this conceit, as a 'vestige of childhood tales in which not only humans spoke but other creatures too. Mountains and streams.' 'I imagine she speaks to me still, what's inside her, how to get it out,' replies Hearst. Continuing his false flattery, Jack points out that such a privileged conversation can be isolating – a fact that Hearst seems to take pride in, when he tells Bullock after Alma has signed over her gold mine to him, 'You mistake for fear what is in fact preoccupation. I'm having a conversation you cannot hear.' In the audio commentary on this scene, Milch remarks 'that's what Rupert Murdoch tells himself in the mirror each morning'. Several times in the transcripts, Hearst was compared to Murdoch as a contemporary example of a similar figure, vastly powerful and yet sequestered beyond the ordinary conversations of the rest of us. Murdoch might be shorthand for the kind of power that needs a proper humility and sense of scale in order to make our care for one another more than perfunctory gesturing: like Adams taking care of Hawkeye, or Trixie maintaining her friendship with Alma after quitting her job at the bank to make a deposit, or Charlie donating Hickok's bearskin rug to the lovers he must envy.

The third season is also swept over by these ideas of building up versus tearing down the camp. There is plenty of irony to Hearst's secret code for the mercenaries he hires to tear down the place, whom he calls 'bricks'. Langrishe tells the ailing Chesterton that the camp is 'yearning for elevation', and builds a new schoolhouse before starting work on a theatre; Alma opens the camp's first bank. Against this, Hearst vows to tear the place down 'like Gomorrah' and has the dubious achievement of making us feel pity for Farnum after spitting in his face and ordering him not to clean it off. Even the fouling of this grotesque is too much, too alien to our sense of the limits of the camp's depravities. After this, he tells Farnum that he knows the smell of 'human flesh on a spit' because 'it pleased me to find out': the absence of scale has created an appetite for knowledge in excess of all human morality – it is the price of knowing the name of the world in that way.[101]

Several things balance this dark view. Most of all, the involving liveliness of Langrishe's 'amateur night' reminds us creativity can relieve us of the burden of our self in performance, silliness and spectacles of skill. Only the mean-spirited are affronted, as Farnum is when he sees the joy Richardson's juggling stimulates among the audience. Similarly, there is Jane's extraordinary rendition to Joanie of her dream which stands comparison with a Beckett soliloquy for its feeling of sheer emission beyond intellect; it describes a dialogue with Charlie Utter as she moves in the dream through various traumatic events that we too have witnessed as *Deadwood*'s audience: the time Swearengen barged past her to get at Sofia, the moment Hickok is murdered; but also by contrast, the healing sound of the 'Row Row Row Your Boat' nursery rhyme which they sing to the child in the wagon outside the camp, the song which closes the second episode. When in the dream Utter tells her, 'Don't you know the world says its fucking name to us?', it may remind us of the other two figures we have seen the 'earth talk to', Hearst and Wolcott; but the antidote, or balm in the face of such awful knowledge, is in our balancing and moderating the punitive rebukes of the past with the habits, routines and alliances of the here and now that offset them. Of course such habits are hardly inevitably healthful. Jane says she dreamed the dream because Joanie sent for her to escort the schoolchildren, when she was dead drunk in the street; and later they kissed. So everything is recoverable.

But nothing is enough to stop Hearst. In one of the writers' room transcripts, Milch says, 'The deepest intention of the series with multiple storylines is to suggest that the unit of attention properly is not the single individual but individuals in connection with one another.' But by the third season Milch was particularly concerned not to 'pin Al into the corner as a hero' and it is clear that their strategy is to balance his impulses toward civilisation, society and order by showing him commit immoral acts, mostly violent murder. While Al is able to conduct tactical disruption such as, in one of his final 'office' scenes, beating then cold-bloodedly slicing the throat of Barrett, the threat that Hearst could reduce the camp to ruins ultimately stays his hand, arguing against Utter's suggestion that they, following Hickok's policy, strike first. Against Bullock's impatient hand ticking on his holster he says, 'if blood's what it finally comes to, the forest is what they'll find here. Dewy morning's lost its appeal to me. I prefer to wake indoors.' As Hemingway puts it, the 'great thing is to last'.

Al deploys the media against Hearst of course, and we see the early-morning delivery, by Merrick and Blazanov, of the newspaper that publishes Bullock's kindly letter to the family of the Cornish union organiser whom Hearst has had murdered. That it is the written word rather than violent action which is used as a weapon leaves the usually animated central characters somewhat bewildered. Even the letter's author returns home dissatisfied and is mean to his wife; Adams and Dority struggle to explain its meaning to Johnny; and we see Swearengen alone and stunned and silent in his office until Langrishe explains the letter's symbolic potency:

AL: I sit mystified I was moved to endorse it.
LANGRISHE: Mystified Al? At proclaiming a law beyond law to a
man who's beyond law himself? It's a publication invoking a decency
whose scrutiny applies to him as to all his fellows. I call that strategy
cunningly sophisticated, befitting and becoming the man who sits
before me.   ('Unauthorized Cinnamon')

The public embarrassment to Hearst when the letter is
published prompts him to instruct the leader of his newly arrived
pistoleros, Barrett, to beat Merrick savagely in his office. (He does
stand it like a man this time.) Hearst creates an impasse in the drama
of the show which, in its final episodes seems tilted across scales of
conflict, with the self-made merchant on his balcony on one side of
the thoroughfare and the mining magnate on his improvised veranda
on the other. On these scales we can balance Swearengen's
accomplishment – the *Deadwood* camp itself, around which he
escorts Langrishe bursting with pride – against, on the other side,
Hearst's implacable but obscurely defined Evil. The muddy main
street is the setting, stage or medium in which their conflict gets
played out.

Swearengen's strategy is ultimately to refuse Hearst the
satisfaction of action: after Alma is shot at on her way to the bank in a
scheme to provoke a violent response from Ellsworth and Bullock, his
forces would surely win. That act animates the camp into action – even
Swearengen leaps from his balcony to protect her. Hearst now aspires to
the role Al occupied at the end of the second season – a director of all
action. Al's scheme to deny him this effectively acknowledges the
audience's appetite for decisive, meaningful action and names it an
infantile impatience:

165

We want his piss pot's play hours occupied by confusion and grievance. We
want him sitting, sulking like a three-year-old whose toys won't do his
bidding … .Hearst's not to see he's had half a fucking cunt hair's effect on
any of the comings and goings in this camp.   ('A Constant Throb')

Like the story about the schoolhouse tree, *Deadwood* seeks to tutor us to stay our impatience and hurry in seeking to know 'the name of the world': the end and meaning of the story that violent action quickly makes apparent. It takes the murder of Ellsworth to get things working to Hearst's satisfaction: 'the camp is galvanised. People scurry about. They've tasks to perform. They feel important,' he says watching the thoroughfare from his window.

It is in the disruption of friendship, loyalty and habit that Hearst wreaks his most devastating destruction on the camp. In one of the most poignant scenes, we see Aunt Lou teaching Richardson how to prepare and bag a ham for smoking; suddenly Hearst enters and tells her that Odell has been found dead. We've already seen how much Aunt Lou despises her master, in a brief scene of her winning at Mah-jong in Chinatown, for he is a 'Copperhead', a Democrat who believes black people adore him. Lou runs from his attempt to comfort her into the arms of Richardson. 'I'm sorry mama,' he weeps, as he tries to console her, 'I can't take it, I can't take it,' she bawls.

On the other side of the scales guilt and justified revenge are just as deadly: after Hearst has Ellsworth assassinated and his body taken along the thoroughfare on the back of a cart, Trixie goes to his room, lifts her dress and shoots him in the shoulder. The merely wounded Hearst seeks compensation from Al demanding the life of the woman who shot at him. True to his nature, Al gambles on a deception. Assuming that Hearst would have paid attention to Trixie's body rather than her face he plans to substitute the body of Jen (Jennifer Lutheran) for that of Trixie. If Hearst falls for it, he will stay his forces of revenge on the town.

Jen is the whore we have glimpsed most, after Dolly, in the *Gem*: she is the one we see Johnny teaching to read the morning newspaper, and it is she who makes the brilliant observation to the other whores as the final meeting of the town elders begins: 'Guess if you've got a pussy, even owning a bank don't get you to that table.' Al only chooses her instead of sacrificing Trixie because, as he tells The Chief: 'What's the fucking alternative? I ain't fucking killing her that sat nights with me sick and taking slaps to her mug that were some less than fucking fair.' Burns, who is in love with Jen, discovers that he is unable to murder her; trying to ready the courage to do so, he stands with her in front of a blank wall and talks of the society of ants within: 'the soldier ants and the worker ants and the whore ants to fuck the soldier and the workers … baby ants … everyone's got a task to hew to Jen'. This is an impoverished model of organic society, bereft of the morality or love that stills Burns's hand on the knife; teaching can only go so far with deception. It is left to Swearengen to cut her throat in a scene we do not see.

The final deception rests on Hearst's inability to tell one human being from another. Hearst and his mercenaries crowd into the room in the *Gem*, where Jen is lying murdered in a wooden coffin. Swearengen, alone, armed with his knife, has instructed the others:

> We show united in the prelude when he's making his entrance and the fucking like. Comes to viewing the body, I stand for virtue alone. The deception failing, I'll make a pass at him with my blade. In the aftermath, play the lie as mine, knowing I speak of you in heaven. Others owe thought to the future – their thinking straightforward don't come that naturally to.
>
> ('Tell Him Something Pretty')

Swearengen is willing to sacrifice his own life for the future of the camp. Satisfied that Jen is the one, Hearst makes to leave, wiping his bloodied boots on the floorboards. Later, in the final shot, we see Swearengen, in a motif long established as one of the skills, like 'close-in' knife work, in which he had pride, scrubbing the floor. He is uncharacteristically alone, but characteristically in discourse with himself and with the objects that remain: the whisky bottle, the safe, the blood on the floorboards, Jen's coffin.

The third season shows the life-giving nature of art, even as it depicts life's brutal extinguishing: *Deadwood* discovers such rich entanglements of human despair, loss, joy, hope in the new characters it introduces, that we cannot look at Al's scrubbing of Jen's blood from the floor with anything but mixed feelings. This season ends, as did the others, with the departure from the town of those forces that would disrupt it, but the tone is vastly different to the previous endings.[102] We are left with the massed forces of Hearst and Swearengen's 'ragtag collection' of hires (including Wu's men) ranged against one another; but the only bloodshed comes from Tolliver's unprovoked, inexplicable fatal stabbing of Leon, who bleeds to death on the balcony while the new whore Janine/Stupid bears her naked breasts at him in order to prevent Tolliver from slaughtering her as well. Perhaps Tolliver, now recruited to be in charge of Hearst's 'other than mining interests in the camp', feels his irrevocable separation from its momentum and aims his gun at Hearst in a parody of the real sacrifice that Swearengen is able to offer (although he cannot know of its detail)? There is no certain reason for his actions but it answers our experience of the world tilting off its axis as forces we can barely grasp muster around us. *Deadwood*'s indirections and misdirections leave us doubting that there is any hand in control and that is how we come to share the chaotic experience of these characters.

168

What we do know is that, with Tolliver at the harness, the camp's fortunes are in peril once again: compare his response with Al's to the news that Cochran is a 'lunger' (i.e. has tuberculosis). To cultivate the public spirit, one needs strong, inspirational leadership capable of animating society with words. Tolliver murders his workers; Hearst intimidates his with the sheer force of his power and money. But even Star and Utter (and to some extent Jane and Joanie), end up taking orders from Al; they 'hew to him', not because they like him but because he offers the best leadership for those who want to flourish within a successful settlement. On the other hand, a single leader cannot hold back the spinning of the world at large. The elections we see taking place in Sturgis thus quickly become an irrelevant backdrop – we see that Hearst has bought them, just as he promises to Merrick to have his people set up a newspaper 'to lie the other way'. More ominously, in the thoroughfare crowded with the massed combatants, we see in the distance Star and Trixie running, clinging to one another: her shame at having caused the death of Jen, coming on the cusp of their mutual agreement to care for Sofia in the event of Alma's death. Of all the couples in the camp, they represented the best hope for its renewal. And there remains hope: Hearst has gone and Tolliver is probably no match for the forces that remain. When one of Hearst's vicious pistoleros makes monkey gestures at the Nigger General as he comes to vote, Rutherford, the shit-stirring regular at Nuttall's saloon (played with conviction by the screenwriter Ted Mann) is usefully on hand to remind any who would listen 'that the right to vote shall not be abridged or denied, fifteenth amendment to the US Constitution'; when the Pinkerton makes a gesture indicating that the Nigger General may later face a lynching, Utter warns him off: 'If he don't make it you'll be eating your spuds running till I hunt you down.' There are no guarantees: but his action suggests that in *Deadwood*, while 'vile injustice may flourish it cannot rest content'.[103] Behind them we see Richardson, without his protective antlers, and dressed up neatly with help from Aunt Lou, proudly drop his vote into the ballot box.

169

9 Wu, Cocksuckers

In a murderous time,
the heart breaks and breaks
and lives by breaking.

Stanley Kunitz, 'The Testing-Tree'

Late in 2008, two years after *Deadwood* ended, a new DVD box set called *Deadwood: The Complete Series* was published. It contained all the riches of the previous series box sets – the behind-the-scenes featurettes, the little documentary histories of the town, the lively audio commentaries from the cast and crew, all the 'extras' that now seem to be essential in our consumption of fine television. For this edition, there was a bonus disc containing a twenty-minute film called 'The Meaning of Endings: David Milch on the Conclusion of *Deadwood*'. In this sad piece, Milch, wearing sunglasses and dressed in black, wanders around the empty exterior sets on the Gene Autry ranch, pointing to the naked buildings in the sunshine – the ones that served as the *Gem*, Bullock and Star's hardware store, the *Grand Central Hotel*, etc. – and speaks with characteristic eloquence about the stories they would have told had they been given the chance: 'I find all of this infinitely depressing,' he says. 'The whole idea of the ending of something as being its source of meaning is what I find a little problematic,' continues Milch and speculates that the security that regular storytelling offers – say, the staging of Hickok's murder in the real town of Deadwood 'fourteen times a day' – is a comfort realists must forego: we are not entitled to 'a meaningful and coherent summarising of something which never concludes'. His wanderings are intercut with behind-the-scenes footage that reinforces the sense of happy times past on the set, made possible only by the 'combination of corporate and personal imperatives', and 'coincidence of separate interests' that allows any art form requiring a mass industrial base to flourish. The sequence concludes with a single shot that pans with Milch as he exits frame left, only to halt its movement on the figure of Wu – or Keone Young dressed as Wu – watching him leave.

In a characteristic gesture of generosity, Milch had the actor appear in the sequence in costume in order that he receive a fee but the gesture goes beyond itself and reminds us of the ways in which resentment, menace and rebuke can be made available as feelings to be experienced by withholding comment, letting the viewers' sensibilities populate the stage that has been prepared for them. Earlier Milch claimed that 'all of Chinatown was intended as a venue for storytelling to show the people who were invisible to what history takes to be the main story of a place' – but here as there, we rarely hear their voices. Instead, throughout the *mise en scène* the Chinese workers are mostly onlookers, the manifestation of forces that are powerful but silent. Their looks are also stages for the projection of meaning: when Steve is washing himself, after Nuttall pours a spittoon over his head, he rebukes the Chinese men watching him as if he knew what they were thinking; but their silent faces merely reflect his alienated thoughts back to him. The Chinese people we frequently glimpse in the background of the town represent the labour on which the excesses and violence of Deadwood is built; in this way, the work speaks to a very contemporary sense of America as a decadent nation financed by Asian value-creation. Wu himself is a device to illustrate the fundamental symbolic struggle to communicate meaning – there are no subtitles to his speech – and the few words he has (especially one of them), display a range of shadings and gradation of meaning according to their context. Like Richardson's antler religion, Wu's grasping for communicative sense stages the improvisation of the fundamental, necessary aspects of human society –

belief and language. In turn, Al's (and, later, Johnny's) proficiency in interpretation points out to us our common need – often stimulated by personal appetites and interests – to understand. We are drawn to Wu not only because of Keone Young's mesmerising performance, but because of the way he and the other Chinese are constantly abused as instruments, means, to the ends of the whites in the camp. We experience it as a form of slavery, never more so than when, in an office scene, Al refuses to support Wu in his battle with Mr Lee, prompted by his outrage at the burning of the Chinese girls: 'Swedgin doesn't give a fuck! Back to Chink's Alley Wu!' Dority, Johnny and Adams shuffle their feet, feeling, as we do (and before Al explains to us all his tactics) the shame of loyalty betrayed.

Along with other cast members, notably W. Earl Brown and Jim Beaver, Young was a prominent voice in the online message boards when a furore erupted once it was known that *Deadwood* had not been financed for a fourth season. The show was never officially 'cancelled', but was rather left, in Tom Nuttall's words, 'to die the death of a thousand cuts', with cast contracts not being renewed, but sets put in storage as if for a later time. The precise timeline is unclear, but it seems that in spring 2006, as production on the third-season episodes was being completed (somewhat later than in the previous two years), negotiations surrounding the fourth season encountered 'difficulties' and 'complications'. This was partly due to the show's success: Milch was at the time contracted to a five-year development deal with Paramount; in working with HBO on *Deadwood* this meant that foreign sales – and overseas DVD revenues – went to Paramount. That obligation was due to end with the fourth season and it made financial sense to lessen HBO's costs on an expensive series (estimated at $5 million per episode); Chris Albrecht, president of HBO (who was later to have problems of his own) offered Milch a short season of six episodes – with the intention to go back to twelve for the fifth year – which Milch rejected, on the grounds that it would catastrophically compromise their storytelling range and depth. By May 2006, it had been agreed to make two two-hour movies instead.[104]

Deadwood had sunk its roots deep. The critical acclaim the show received was not simply in the outstanding industry recognition (it was nominated for over thirty awards in the US alone, winning ten of them), but in the way the show immediately gripped the critics and scholars, who recognised its value as extraordinary television, and also the way its background artists sometimes included media stars wanting to be included in the action.[105] The justified outcry from the cast and the 500 or so crew, many of whom had made financial decisions based on earlier assurances that there would be another season, and of course, fans, became a campaign to 'Save Deadwood', where one word, in relation to HBO's behaviour, was predictably prominent. The show was not the first, nor the last to suffer such a fate (one thinks of *Carnivàle* and *Veronica Mars*, 2004–7), and it was particularly unfortunate that Milch himself was the target of some anger for allegedly abandoning interest in the show in order to pursue the surfing *noir* drama which he later developed with Kem Nunn as *John from Cincinnati*. Nothing could be further from the truth; speaking in 2007, Milch describes his utter devastation at the sudden and arbitrary nature of the cancellation which offered him no chance to get the show into shape for an ending:

173

> In the aftermath of losing something which was very precious to me … *Deadwood* … I thought … would be the last work I'd do, because then I wanted to go back to teaching. For reasons absolutely extraneous, from my point of view, to what would or wouldn't have justified keeping that on the air, that show is gone.[106]

A murderous time indeed. Whatever the reason or truth behind the failure to restore the show – and we should note Deadwood's tutelage to us to season our thoughts in their most potent proportion – it formed another milestone on what has since become a series of strategic and creative wobbles at HBO. And it must be a pitiful world for those that cling onto whatever justification remains for the show's termination. Recent noises from HBO executives suggest that a lesson has been learned, but that does not make the hurt any less for the artists involved. After Milch called him with the grim news, W. Earl Brown remembers,

> I got a tattoo that night, and the whole time I'm getting the tattoo, I'm focusing on the pain. Have you ever gotten a tattoo? You take your mind elsewhere so you don't think about how much it hurts. But not that night. It was like, *bleed*. Fucking *hurt*.[107]

The problem with the movie solution was that it implied altering the Aristotelian organisation of time where a single day was the container for most of its dramatic action in most episodes. The proposed two films were not made but sketches and ideas for them exist, notably those found on Milch's own DVD commentaries (including the 1879 fire that razed the town to the ground, the flood, the contamination of the drinking water by Hearst's mines, and the arrival of John Rockefeller's father as medicine man/quack doctor). Some of the script outlines offer wonderful ideas: the *Grand Central* as Aunt Lou's restaurant, a changing of the guard with Dan taking Al's place on the balcony; the expansion of Chinatown, Joanie as schoolteacher. These sketches for stories are set a few years later and all involve a diminishment of Swearengen's power; one suggestion was to have him leave with Trixie after they burn the town to the ground concluding with a literary image where we have Swearengen, like his real-life counterpart, dying alone in a Denver street, light snow falling over him. One hopes that one day the films or something else (musical? opera?) may yet be realised. It is for generations to come to discover the disappointment that the exquisite ending of season three leads us forward to something that has no conclusion, its shape unfinished.

This is a tough story– *Deadwood* tough – for any artist, but it is important not to read back into the show its conditions of cancellation. Hearst as a corporate Evil versus the solidarity of a tightly knit organic group of course mirrors to some extent the relationship between a media corporation and the production companies who work for it. But the Hearst storyline was established and mostly shot well before there was any hint of cancellation. And *Deadwood*, in its 'glow/haze' associational approach, warns against those who would seek clarity at the cost of suggestion. *Deadwood*, as Jen might point out if her throat was not cut, is hardly unproblematically about the virtuous Team Swearengen against Team Hearst, any more than it is a neoliberal celebration of individualism or a liberal rant against Murdoch and capitalism. Good art rarely divides that neatly.

Since it was never concluded, how can we talk about its legacy as a classic? I hope I have given a flavour here that may be another early step in the critical work of approximating an adequate evaluation of a show that should continue to exercise its grip on the future of any criticism interested in achievement in television art, or in any storytelling art.

One of the ways in which it was recognised at the time as innovatory was its contemplation of the role of language in the development of civilisation. Its achievement in this respect is in posing the narrative of human settlement as a struggle to transcend the illusions of our separateness, illusions fostered by our talking to ourselves critically as 'judge and jury'. The medium in which we can overcome these self-renewing barriers is the strange energy form of language itself, a symbolic clawing and carving out of a meaningful space for ourselves in the fabric of the social which it in turn constructs. The show does this dramatically by having as its setting a world where practical desire and the establishment of human law are terms in a settlement which is fuelled and propelled by deep individual and obscure drives and impulses – obscure to their owners, and their creators, – so that, as an audience, we are constantly aware of background forces operating simultaneously on the vivid surface textures we see, like the blurred blobs of light we see in the *bokeh* behind the foreground action.

175

It is easy of course as well as quite fun, to get caught up in the immediacy of *Deadwood*'s saucy and scandalous language: one website estimated a cumulative total of just under 3,000 or one and a half FPM (fucks per minute).[108] But the true source of its language springs from American literature and, as I noted in the first chapter, specifically the work of Herman Melville:

> Passion, and passion in its profoundest, is not a thing demanding a palatial stage whereon to play its part. Down among the groundlings, among the beggars and rakers of the garbage, profound passion is enacted. And the circumstances that provoke it, however trivial or mean, are no measure of its power.[109]

This language and the elements of passion it locates 'among the groundlings' sit squarely in the idiom, sentiment and worldview of *Deadwood*. It has also been described as Shakespearean, and it probably earns something of that accolade not least because of its range of ambition to compass the human, and in the way it discovers surprising aspects and dimensions of the beauty of the human heart – the one that lives, and grows, by breaking and breaking – in the complex antagonisms of law and desire. In this way, it is redolent of *Measure for Measure*; in his wonderful account of the play, E. M. W. Tillyard, talking about Isabella's poetic speech on human pride argues that it,

176

> Illustrates the truth that in the drama the most powerful general effect comes by way of absorption into the immediate dramatic business, just as writers are most likely to speak to all ages when most sensitive to the spiritual climate of their own.[110]

This could equally apply to Milch and the other creators of *Deadwood*, who have produced a work that speaks in a specific language, historical setting and genre, yet which reaches out beyond itself. In doing so, it does not reject or sublate the vulgar commercial culture it depicts in order to point to timeless values that transcend the material world; rather, it discovers 'down among the groundlings' the currents of light and lift in which the human spirit inheres in its collective striving for solidarity, peace and calm. The filthy joy of the series lies in the prominence of its immediate vulgar materiality; its language digs through this coarse environment of blood, breasts, cocks and cash and builds into an entire world whose raw immediacy forces us to share its aspirations by binding us to intimate relationships with its vivid characters. As the product of a supposedly vulgar medium, *Deadwood* itself demonstrates the transcendent possibilities of material mass culture.

As the credits roll on its episodes, *Deadwood* plays music selected from a range of styles and periods, all twentieth century, some of them folksy like Mike Seeger's 'Snake Baked a Hoe Cake', others seeming to comment, however obscurely, on the action just concluded (the best of these choices, for this purpose, is Bob Dylan's 'Not Dark Yet' played at the end of 'A Lie Agreed Upon, Part I'). But as is so often the case with *Deadwood*, what comes first, a product of intuition perhaps, establishes a resonance across the work as a whole: Michael Hurley's 'Hog of the Forsaken' is played over the credits for the first episode (as well as the tenth). It is a strange blend of acid folk and comic mysticism with lyrics that speak of a mythic pig, 'the pork of crime', a figure and a sound which seem rooted in the past and yet equally have the quality of coming to us from the distorted culture of the future, 'He sings of these and those times as well as times to go.' *Deadwood*'s textures are soaked in the past and yet the language and inner lives of its characters reach out to us as somehow from the future. Wu's pigs are used both comically (Al to Farnum: 'I will profane your fucking remains E . B. … Gabriel's trumpet will produce you from the ass of a pig') and to underline the far darker matter of what we leave behind; Joanie is repulsed by the sight of the pigs munching the bodies of Flora and Miles, perhaps because it represents their total erasure from history, a terrible condition she herself sometimes aspires to. Like the Hog of the Forsaken, *Deadwood*, in its blending of modern and old sounds, sometimes seems not a raw depiction of times past, but a lesson in how we might reconstitute ourselves in the devastation of a future world.

177

That reconstitution would be cultivated by these fine characters, who have a thirst for talk as well as drink. In what is a tragic aside during 'The Meaning of Endings,' Milch comments:

> I'm grateful beyond words for the experience of working on *Deadwood* … I would hope that the continuous present which is the imaginative experience of participating in the watching of these shows imports no truth beyond itself. That's what's always been the true joy for me in writing …

178

The Chinese look on from the edges; Wu watches Joanie watching Flora's remains being eaten by his pigs

and I try not to think about it before I do it and I try not to think about it after it's done ... that's why I have a good chance of drinking this afternoon and I haven't had a drink in nearly ten years.

Like another great work of American fiction, *The Great Gatsby* – also written when its creator was on the wagon – this is a narrative saturated

179

David Milch talks about endings on the empty set.

with depictions of the consumption of booze, with shot glasses chinking down and arms pouring whisky bottles with the practised regularity of a metronome. This is the social drinking that is the lubrication for, and a necessary part of the adjustments of, a settlement that brings those with more moral integrity like Utter into Al's flock. In the penultimate episode, 'The Catbird Seat', with Alma ensconced in Al's office after being shot at, we see Jack Langrishe, convivial as ever, finally get to hand Charlie a shot glass in the bar of the *Gem* (the first is snatched by Al), who sits down next to Dan. 'Thought you was near pitching a tent and setting up housekeeping over there on that first step,' the latter says to him. Adams snorts with laughter. 'You sound like a pig my cousin ran off with,' says Utter, friendly. 'Get another?' And they drink on, ready to face the world together.

Notes

1 *The Real Deadwood – Historical Featurette* [Disc 6], *Deadwood: The Complete Series* DVD (HBO, 2008).

2 Karl Marx and Friedrich Engels, 'The Communist Manifesto', in Irving Howe (ed.), *Essential Works of Socialism* (New Haven, CT and London: Yale University Press, 1976).

3 George Simmel, *The Philosophy of Money*, 3rd edn (London and New York: Routledge, 2004), pp. 128–9.

4 Robert Pippin, *Hollywood Westerns and American Myth: The Importance of Howard Hawks and John Ford for Political Philosophy* (New Haven, CT: Yale University Press, 2010); Jim Kitses, *Horizons West: Directing the Western from John Ford to Clint Eastwood*, new edn (London: BFI, 2004).

5 See Kitses, *Horizons West*, p. 314.

6 'Herman Melville', in Cleanth Brooks, R. W. B. Lewis and Robert Penn Warren (eds), *American Literature: The Makers and the Making, Book B 1826 to 1861* (New York: St Martin's Press, 1973), p. 820.

7 David Milch, *Deadwood: Stories of the Black Hills* (New York: Bloomsbury, 2006).

8 Cormac McCarthy, *Blood Meridian* (London: Picador, 1990), p. 330; Jimmy Flynn (Titus Welliver) in episode 8 of *Big Apple* (CBS, 2001).

9 Donald Sassoon, *The Culture of the Europeans: From 1800 to the Present* (London: HarperCollins, 2006), p. 346.

10 The mountain-building process, known as the Trans-Hudson orogeny, was the event that formed the North American craton. Cratons are the oldest and thickest parts of the earth's crust and their deep lithospheric roots extend for miles into the earth's mantle. *Deadwood* could hardly boast a location with any securer footing in the world.

11 Shelby Foote speaking in *The Civil War* (Ken Burns, PBS, 1990).

12 Pippin, *Hollywood Westerns and American Myth*, p. 24.

13 Edward Lazarus, *Black Hills/White Justice: The Sioux Nation versus the United States 1775 to the Present* (Lincoln: University of Nebraska Press, 1999), p. 71.

14 Lazarus, *Black Hills*, p. 72.

15 Lazarus, *Black Hills*, p. 76.

16 The real Merrick was editor of the *Black Hills Pioneer*. Changing the name of the paper allows the show to inscribe and display the name of the town on its sign, absorbing the title of the show into the background *mise en scène*.

17 This is an ongoing issue: Ward Churchill sees the Black Hills (Paha Sapa) land disputes as 'a lens through which all such Indian–Government conflicts can be viewed and more readily understood', *The Struggle for Land: Native North American Resistance to Genocide* (San Francisco, CA: City Lights Books, 2002), p. 114.

18 Ralph Waldo Emerson in his essay 'History' remarks, ' "What is history", said Napoleon, "but a fable agreed upon?", *Essays* (London: Macmillan, 1911), p. 10. Sometimes *Deadwood* is obsessive about pursuing the origins of historical myth, as in its dramatisation of Captain Massie's 'dead man's hand' story.

19 Jeffrey P. Jones, 'Acknowledgements', in Gary R. Edgerton and Jeffrey P. Jones (eds), *The Essential HBO Reader* (Lexington:

University Press of Kentucky, 2008), p. viii. See also Edgerton's chapter, 'Introduction: A Brief History of HBO' in the same book.

20 The exception is of course *Carnivàle* (HBO, 2003–5).

21 Robert Blanco, *USA Today*, 18 March 2004.

22 See Roger Catlin, 'No Place for Tenderfoots: Deadwood Wouldn't Take Kindly to Old West', *Hartford Courant*, 17 March 2004. The interview by Terry Gross was on the *Fresh Air* show, NPR, 25 March 2005.

23 *Tavis Smiley*, 31 March 2004; Milch goes on to note that: 'I think that the irresponsible, promiscuous use of profanity and titillation is something that is a genuine issue in society, and the way that it is being handled on television is because every form of behaviour is being turned into an article of commerce.'

24 Pippin, *Hollywood Westerns and American Myth*, p. 19.

25 The document cites Thomas Docherty, *Pre-Code Hollywood* (New York: Columbia University Press, 1999) and Kevin Brownlow, *War, the West and the Wilderness* (New York: Alfred A. Knopf, 1978), H. L Mencken's *The American Language*, 4th edn (New York: Knopf, 1936), Daniel Boorstin, *The Americans* (Harmondsworth: Penguin, 1969) and the American memory project called 'California as I Saw It: First-Person Narratives of California's Early Years, 1849–1900' among its many sources.

26 Pippin, *Hollywood Westerns and American Myth*, p. 163.

27 György Markus, 'Lukács, György', in Michael Kelly (ed.), *Encyclopedia of Aesthetics*, *Vol. 3* (New York: Oxford University Press, 1998), p. 170. Markus is discussing Lukács's *The Specificity of the Aesthetic* (1963).

28 See Heather Havilresky, 'The Man behind Deadwood', *Salon.com*, 17 July 2005 and Mark Singer, 'The Misfit: How David Milch Got from *NYPD Blue* to *Deadwood* by Way of an Epistle of St Paul', *New Yorker*, 14 February 2005.

29 These details can be found in Milch's typically candid accounts of his life scattered in David Milch and Bill Clark, *True Blue: The Real Stories behind* NYPD Blue, rev. edn (New York: Avon Books, 1997). The summer camp was the aptly named Camp Paradox.

30 See Blake Bailey, *A Tragic Honesty: The Life and Work of Richard Yates* (New York: Picador, 2003).

31 Quoted in Joseph Blotner, *Robert Penn Warren: A Biography* (New York: Random House, 1997), p. 381.

32 See the correspondence collected in James A. Grimshaw, Jr (ed.), *Cleanth Brooks and Robert Penn Warren: A Literary Correspondence* (Columbia and London: University of Missouri Press, 1998) for an account of Milch's painstaking work for, and value to, his teachers.

33 In his acknowledgment to Milch, Lewis writes 'I owe Mr Milch even more for the wealth of suggestions he made out of his extensive literary, psychological, medical and legal knowledge', *Edith Wharton: A Biography* (New York: Fromm International Publishing, 1975), p. 573.

34 This became Lewis's *The Jameses: A Family Narrative* (New York: Farrar, Straus & Giroux, 1991).

35 For an account of this tragic event, see Milch's interview with David Thorburn, 'Television's Great Writer', *MIT World*, 20 April 2006: <mitworld.mit.edu/video/383>.

36 *Big Apple*'s cast included Kim Dickens, Titus Welliver and Pasha Lychnikoff who were to feature prominently in *Deadwood*.

37 Interesting as that show was, and happy *Deadwood* was born out of its presence, I cannot be alone in wanting to see what Milch's version of Rome might have been.
38 '*Deadwood* Creator Has a Way with Words', *Los Angeles Times*, 19 March 2004.
39 See for example Sean O'Sullivan's excellent essay, 'Old, New, Borrowed, Blue: *Deadwood* and Serial Fiction', in David Lavery (ed.), *Reading Deadwood*: *A Western to Swear By* (New York and London: I. B Tauris, 2006).
40 This is based on a real incident, the killing of Charles Metz, his wife and a cook in April 1876 purportedly by road agents *and* Indians led by Persimmon Bill (not 'Phil' as in Milch's version). The children are a fictional addition.
41 The Pinkertons was a private security agency established in 1850 by Allan Pinkerton. It tended to be hired by the rich to protect their interests.
42 Horace Newcomb also makes the Miltonic connection in 'Deadwood', in Edgerton and Jones, *The Essential HBO Reader*.
43 See Jason Jacobs, 'Al Swearengen, Philosopher King', in Lavery, *Reading Deadwood*.
44 Mention of Abilene would be hurtful for Hickok since this is the place where he accidentally killed one of his deputies.
45 Emerson, 'Self-Reliance', *Essays*, p. 39.
46 This is the phrase Milch uses to describe one of his egregious juvenile acts, see 'Idea of the Writer', 12 December 2007, <theideaofthewriter.blogspot.com>.
47 The music is 'Iguazu' from Gustavo Santaolalla from his album *Ronrocco* (1998).
48 John Jones, *On Aristotle and Greek Tragedy* (London: Chatto and Windus, 1962), p. 29.

49 Joseph Conrad, *Heart of Darkness* (Harmondsworth: Penguin, 1973), p. 8. This is one of Milch's many literary quotes often brought up in the writers' room.
50 See Susan Neiman, *Moral Clarity* (London: Bodley Head, 2009), p. 171.
51 Milch, *Deadwood*, p. 213.
52 Perhaps there are echoes here of Emerson's 'Where do we find ourselves? In a series of which we do not know the extremes, and believe that it has none' in his essay, 'Experience', *Essays*.
53 Milch, *Deadwood*, p. 213.
54 Robert Penn Warren, 'Homage to Theodore Dreiser', in John Burt (ed.), *The Collected Poems of Robert Penn Warren* (Baton Rouge: Louisiana State University Press, 1998).
55 The corruption is so fundamental to Deadwood that the Argentinian title for the show is *Deadwood, Pueblo corrupto* ('Deadwood, Corrupt People').
56 David Milch production discussion 28 May 2008.
57 William James, *Principles of Psychology, Vol. 1* (New York: Cosimo, 2007), p. 488; Milton, *L'Allegro*.
58 For a while the HBO website showcased her production and costume designs.
59 'On Deadwood Set, History Comes Alive: HBO's Hit Western Is Built on a Mountain of Research', 3 March 2005, MSNBC, <today.msnbc.msn.com/id/7081175/ns/today-entertainment>.
60 Edward Buscombe, *The Searchers* (London: BFI, 2000), p. 64.
61 Since it merely describes 'the character of cinema' what counts as 'cinematic' is constantly changing.
62 Glennon, who died shortly after the final season aired, was the son of Bert Glennon the cinematographer for, among many others, Westerns such as *Stagecoach*

183

(1939), *Drums along the Mohawk* (1939), *Rio Grande* (1950) as well as some television Westerns.

63 They also developed their own blog which is archived here: <deadwood.blog.com>.

64 E. M. Forster, *Aspects of the Novel* (Aylesbury: Pelican Books, 1974), pp. 78–9.

65 Farnum eventually seems to achieve this sense of entitlement in the closing moments of the final episode when we see him standing on Hearst's balcony, arms akimbo like – as Ted Mann's script indicates – 'Mussolini'.

66 Singer, 'The Misfit'.

67 This included rodeo stars Gary Leffew and Monty Henson who plays Silas Adams's sidekick Hawkeye.

68 O'Sullivan, 'Old, New, Borrowed, Blue, pp. 119–20.

69 See Deborah Thomas, *Beyond Genre: Melodrama, Comedy and Romance in Hollywood Films* (Moffat: Cameron & Hollis, 2000).

70 See the interview with Molly Parker in Milch, *Deadwood*. According to Milch, 'I gave Molly Alice James's diary … . How would you like to be the youngest child in the James family? And the only girl.'

71 *Bokeh* is the Japanese word for out-of-focus elements in a shot.

72 Compare to the final battle in *Lorna Doone* which shares a primeval setting.

73 For a sensible account of both films, see Stanley Cavell, *Contesting Tears: The Hollywood Melodrama of the Unknown Woman* (Chicago, IL: University of Chicago Press, 1996).

74 See *The Idea of the Writer* website, <theideaofthewriter.blogspot.com>.

75 The first reports of gold in the area came from the Belgian Catholic Father Pierre-John De Smet, a missionary working among the Sioux in the region.

76 For an account of this in postwar US literature, see Amy Hungerford, *Postmodern Belief: American Literature and Religion since 1960* (Princeton, NJ: Princeton University Press, 2010).

77 Swearengen is well aware of his power: he jokes he'd fantasised about setting up a specialist brothel in Manchester where he would hang upside down in the corner like a bat.

78 There were plans for a storyline that included the problems with the water supply for the town being poisoned by the tailings from mining work.

79 Steven Peacock provides an excellent reading of this moment in 'Borders and Boundaries in *Deadwood*', in Christine Cornea (ed.), *Genre and Performance: Film and Television* (Manchester: Manchester University Press, 2010).

80 We might reflect here on the aptronymic and onomatopoeaic wonder of the names of the show: the obscene Swearengen, Cochran a medic who tends chiefly to human genitals, Trixie the whore, Bullock, a powerful force driven by animality and Cy, the sad lonely pimp, isolated by his implacable misogyny.

81 Milch, *Deadwood*, p. 169.

82 This is a brilliant decision, in fact a reversal of the initial thinking which was to show the 'joyless cynicism' of Wolcott; making him available to the sense of that joy means his tragedy strikes deeper.

83 In the writers' room transcript Milch says, 'make it as close to fucking Auschwitz as you can'.

84 This is Jack Langrishe's phrase from his stage speech to Claudia in the final episode.

85 This is Milch's phrase in 'The Meaning of Endings: David Milch on the Conclusion of *Deadwood*', DVD Boxed Set, Bonus Disc.

86 Emerson, 'Experience', pp. 343–4.

87 Steven Peacock develops this idea of individuality and type in 'Borders and Boundaries in *Deadwood*'.

88 The service is led by Andy Cramed, also risen from the dead; as it concludes, he steps backwards into a puddle, a tiny moment of baptism.

89 This is Milch's appropriation, which he often quotes, of Herman Melville's definition of great poetry; the relevant line can be found in the poem, 'The Conflict of Convictions': 'I know a wind in purpose strong/It spins *against* the way it drives.'

90 Milch, *Deadwood*, p. 91.

91 This shift from the loyalties of blood and kinship ties to agile forms of adult solidarity is of course a central part of the history of our civilisation. See Francis Fukuyama, *The Origins of Political Order* (New York: Farrar, Straus & Giroux, 2011).

92 Mose effectively replaces William as a fixture of the camp.

93 Milch, *Deadwood*, p. 70.

94 The writers' room transcripts indicate more was to be made of the schoolchildren in the show.

95 Charles Northend, *Dictation Exercises Containing Many Words of Common Use Whose Orthography Is Difficult* (New York: A. S Barnes, 1851), p. 15.

96 Bailey, *A Tragic Honesty*, p. x.

97 'Q&A with Cast and Creative Team', Bonus Disc, *Deadwood: The Complete Series* DVD.

98 See Lewis, *The Jameses*, p. 441.

99 Indian agents were usually white men authorised to act on behalf of the US government in dealing with Native Americans; typically this would involve significant siphoning off of funds.

100 We also see two other women involved in undefined ways with Langrishe: Mary, who may be his wife, and is a painter; and Joseanne, a young actress who he installs in his theatre. Claudia's difficulties with Langrishe imply a father–daughter relationship. One additional fine cameo is Gustave the tailor, played by another *NYPD Blue* veteran Gordon Clapp, who brings colourful swatches for Al's stump.

101 The notion of knowing the 'name of the world' in the sense of total knowledge, with all its attendant burdens as well as insights seems to come from Robert Penn Warren's work, specifically the poem, 'American Portrait: Old Style', as well as his novel *A Place to Come To* (New York: Random House, 1977).

102 See Sean O'Sullivan, 'Reconnoitering the Rim: Thoughts on *Deadwood* and Third Seasons', in Pat Harrigan and Noah Wardrip-Fruin (eds), *Third Person: Authoring and Exploring Vast Narratives* (Cambridge, MA: MIT Press, 2009).

103 Stanley Cavell, 'The Avoidance of Love', *Must We Mean What We Say?* (Cambridge: Cambridge University Press, 1976), p. 309.

104 See Denise Martin, 'Deadwood Rides Again', *Variety*, 4 June 2006.

105 Although these tended to be metalhead W. Earl Brown's buddies: Dusty Hill and Billy Gibbons (*ZZ Top*), Lemmy Kilminster (*Motörhead*), Scott Ian (*Anthrax*), can be seen among the background artists in the final episode of season three. Jerry Cantrell (*Alice in Chains*) and Rex Brown (*Pantera*) appear in the first season.

106 USC Lecture, 'Religion, Media and Hollywood', <theideaofthewriter. blogspot.com/ 2008/02/usc-lecture-religion-media-hollywood.html>.

107 Sean O'Neal interview with W. Earl Brown, *The AV Club*, 6 January 2011. Brown quotes HBO executive Michael Lombardo as saying, 'Looking back it was a mistake to stop *Deadwood*.'

108 See <thewvsr.com/deadwood.htm>.

109 Herman Melville, *Billy Budd, Sailor* (Harmondsworth: Penguin Books, 1985), p. 356.

110 E . M . W. Tillyard, *Shakespeare's Problem Plays* (Harmondsworth: Penguin Books, 1970), pp. 136–7.

Bibliography

Bailey, Blake, *A Tragic Honesty: The Life and Work of Richard Yates* (New York: Picador, 2003).

Blotner, Joseph, *Robert Penn Warren: A Biography* (New York: Random House, 1997).

Boorstin, Daniel, *The Americans* (Harmondsworth: Penguin, 1969).

Brooks, Cleanth, R. W. B. Lewis, Robert Penn Warren, *American Literature: The Makers and the Making, Book B 1826 to 1861* (New York: St Martin's Press, 1973).

Brownlow, Kevin, *War, the West and the Wilderness* (New York: Alfred A. Knopf, 1978).

Burt, John (ed.), *The Collected Poems of Robert Penn Warren* (Baton Rouge: Louisiana State University Press, 1998).

Buscombe, Edward, *The Searchers* (London: BFI, 2000).

Catlin, Roger, 'No Place for Tenderfoots: Deadwood Wouldn't Take Kindly to Old West', *Hartford Courant*, 17 March 2004.

Cavell, Stanley, 'The Avoidance of Love', *Must We Mean What We Say?* (Cambridge: Cambridge University Press, 1976).

Cavell, Stanley, *Contesting Tears: The Hollywood Melodrama of the Unknown Woman* (Chicago,IL: University of Chicago Press, 1996).

Churchill, Ward, *The Struggle for Land: Native North American Resistance to Genocide* (San Francisco, CA: City Lights Books, 2002).

Conrad, Joseph, *Heart of Darkness* (Harmondsworth: Penguin, 1973).

Docherty, Thomas, *Pre-Code Hollywood* (New York: Columbia University Press, 1999).

Edgerton, Gary R. and Jeffrey P. Jones (eds), *The Essential HBO Reader* (Lexington: University Press of Kentucky, 2008).

Emerson, Ralph Waldo, *Essays* (London: Macmillan, 1911).

Forster, E. M., *Aspects of the Novel* (Aylesbury: Pelican Books, 1974).

Fukuyama, Francis, *The Origins of Political Order* (New York: Farrar, Straus & Giroux: 2011).

Grimshaw, Jr, James A. (ed.), *Cleanth Brooks and Robert Penn Warren: A Literary Correspondence* (Columbia and London: University of Missouri Press, 1998).

Havilresky, Heather, 'The Man behind Deadwood', *Salon.com*, 17 July 2005.

Hungerford, Amy, *Postmodern Belief: American Literature and Religion since 1960* (Princeton, NJ: Princeton University Press, 2010).

James, William, *Principles of Psychology, Vol. 1* (New York: Cosimo, 2007).

Jones, John, *On Aristotle and Greek Tragedy* (London: Chatto and Windus, 1962).

Kitses, Jim, *Horizons West: Directing the Western from John Ford to Clint Eastwood*, new edn (London: BFI, 2004).

Lavery, David (ed.), *Reading Deadwood: A Western to Swear By* (New York and London: I. B. Tauris, 2006).

Lazarus, Edward, *Black Hills/White Justice: The Sioux Nation versus the United States 1775 to the Present* (Lincoln: University of Nebraska Press, 1999).

Lewis, R. W. B, *Edith Wharton: A Biography* (New York: Fromm International Publishing, 1975).

Lewis. R. W. B., *The Jameses: A Family Narrative* (New York: Farrar, Straus & Giroux, 1991).

Markus, György, 'Lukács, György', in Michael Kelly (ed.), *Encyclopedia of Aesthetics Vol. 3* (New York: Oxford University Press, 1998).

Martin, Denise, 'Deadwood Rides Again', *Variety*, 4 June 2006.

Marx, Karl and Friedrich Engels, 'The Communist Manifesto', in Irving Howe (ed.), *Essential Works of Socialism* (New Haven, CT and London: Yale University Press, 1976).

McCarthy, Cormac, *Blood Meridian* (London: Picador, 1990).

Melville, Herman, *Billy Budd, Sailor* (Harmondsworth: Penguin Books, 1985).

Mencken, H. L., *The American Language*, 4th edn (New York: Knopf, 1936).

Milch, David, *Deadwood: Stories of the Black Hills* (New York: Bloomsbury, 2006).

Milch, David and Bill Clark, *True Blue: The Real Stories behind NYPD Blue*, rev. edn (New York: Avon Books, 1997).

Neiman, Susan, *Moral Clarity* (London: Bodley Head, 2009).

Northend, Charles, *Dictation Exercises Containing Many Words of Common Use Whose Orthography Is Difficult* (New York: A. S Barnes, 1851).

O'Sullivan, Sean, 'Old, New, Borrowed, Blue: *Deadwood* and Serial Fiction', in David Lavery (ed.), *Reading Deadwood: A Western to Swear By* (New York and London: I. B. Tauris, 2006).

O'Sullivan, Sean, 'Reconnoitering the Rim: Thoughts on *Deadwood* and Third Seasons', in Pat Harrigan and Noah Wardrip-Fruin (eds), *Third Person: Authoring and Exploring Vast Narratives* (Cambridge, MA: MIT Press, 2009).

Peacock, Steven, 'Borders and Boundaries in *Deadwood*', in Christine Cornea (ed.), *Genre and Performance: Film and Television* (Manchester: Manchester University Press, 2010).

Pippin, Robert, *Hollywood Westerns and American Myth: The Importance of Howard Hawks and John Ford for Political Philosophy* (New Haven, CT: Yale University Press, 2010).

Sassoon, Donald, *The Culture of the Europeans: From 1800 to the Present* (London: HarperCollins, 2006).

Simmel, George, *The Philosophy of Money*, 3rd edn (London and New York: Routledge, 2004).

Singer, Mark, 'The Misfit: How David Milch Got from *NYPD Blue* to *Deadwood* by Way of an Epistle of St Paul', *New Yorker*, 14 February 2005.

Thomas, Deborah, *Beyond Genre: Melodrama, Comedy and Romance in Hollywood Films* (Moffat: Cameron & Hollis, 2000).

Thorburn, David, 'Television's Great Writer', *MIT World*, 20 April 2006, <mitworld.mit.edu/video/383>.

Tillyard, E. M. W., *Shakespeare's Problem Plays* (Harmondsworth: Penguin Books, 1970).

Warren, Robert Penn, *A Place to Come to* (New York: Random House, 1977).

Credits

Deadwood
US 2004–6
Created by David Milch
© HBO

executive producers
Gregg Fienberg
David Milch
Mark Tinker
production companies
Red Board Productions
Roscoe Productions
Home Box Office
Paramount Network Television
production design
Maria Caso
costume design
Katherine Jane Bryant
music
David Schwartz (main title)

cast
Timothy Olyphant
Seth Bullock
Ian McShane
Al Swearengen
Molly Parker
Alma Garret
John Hawkes
Sol Star
Paula Malcomson
Trixie
Powers Boothe
Cy Tolliver
Robin Weigert
Jane Cannary
Kim Dickens
Joanie Stubbs
Dayton Callie
Charlie Utter
William Sanderson
E. B. Farnum
W. Earl Brown
Dan Dority
Brad Dourif
Doc Cochran
Titus Welliver
Silas Adams

Sean Bridgers
Johnny Burns
Jim Beaver
Whitney Ellsworth
Jeffrey Jones
A. W. Merrick
Leon Rippy
Tom Nuttall
Keith Carradine
Wild Bill Hickok
Garret Dillahunt
Jack McCall/Francis Wolcott
Geri Jewel
Jewel
Bree Seanna Wall
Sofia Metz
Anna Gunn
Martha Bullock
Gerald McRaney
George Hearst
Peter Jason
Con Stapleton
Larry Cedar
Leon
Franklyn Ajaye
'Nigger General' Fields
Brian Cox
Jack Langrishe
Ralph Richeson
Richardson
Josh Eriksson
William Bullock
Stephen Tobolowsky
Hugo Jarry
Keone Young
Wu
Brent Sexton
Harry Manning
Ray McKinnon
Reverend Smith
Cleo King
Aunt Lou Marchbanks
Ricky Jay
Eddie Sawyer
Pasha Lychnikoff
Blazanov
Richard Gant
Hostetler

Alice Krige
Maddie
Zach Grenier
Andy Cramed
Michael Harney
Steve Fields
Gill Gayle
Soapy
Alan Graf
Captain Turner
Omar Gooding
Odell
Austin Nichols
Morgan Earp
Ashleigh Kizer
Dolly
Jennifer Lutheran
Jen
Pruitt Taylor Vince
Mose Manuel
Sarah Paulson
Miss Isringhausen
Nick Amandos
Jack
Julie Ariola
Countess Berman
Ted Mann
Rutherford
Philip Moon
Lee
Timothy Omundson
Brom Garret
Dean Rader-Duval
Jimmy Irons
Marshall Bell
Magistrate Clagett
Izabella Miko
Carrie
William Russ
Otis Russell
Kristen Bell
Flora
Peter Coyote
General Crook
Gale Harold
Wyatt Earp
Aubrey Morris
Chesterton

Cynthia Ettinger
Claudia
Dennis Christopher
Bellegarde

Broadcast history
Transmitted in the US on the
Home Box Office cable network
on Sunday evenings from
March 2004 to August 2006.
There were three seasons of
twelve episodes.

Season One
21/03/2004 Deadwood
writer: David Milch, director:
Walter Hill
28/03/2004 Deep Water
writer: Malcolm MacRury,
director: Davis Guggenheim
04/04/2004 Reconnoitering
the Rim
writer: Jody Worth, director:
Davis Guggenheim
11/04/2004 Here Was a Man
writer: Elizabeth Sarnoff,
director: Alan Taylor
18/04/2004 The Trial of Jack
McCall
writer: John Belluso, director:
Ed Bianchi
25/04/2004 Plague
writer: Malcolm MacRury,
director: Davis Guggenheim
02/05/2004 Bullock Returns
to the Camp
writer: Jody Worth, director:
Michael Engler
09/05/2004 Suffer the Little
Children
writer: Elizabeth Sarnoff,
director: Dan Minahan
16/05/2004 No Other Sons or
Daughters
writer: George Putnam,
director: Ed Bianchi
23/05/2004 Mister Wu
writer: Bryan McDonald,
director: Dan Minahan
06/06/2004 Jewel's Boot Is
Made for Walking
writer: Ricky Jay, director:
Steve Shill

13/06/2004 Sold under Sin
writer: Ted Mann, director:
Davis Guggenheim

Season Two
06/03/2005 A Lie Agreed
Upon, Part I
writer: David Milch, director:
Ed Bianchi
13/03/2005 A Lie Agreed
Upon, Part II
writer: Jody Worth, director:
Ed Bianchi
20/03/2005 New Money
writer: Elizabeth Sarnoff,
director: Steve Shill
27/03/2005 Requiem for a
Gleet
writer: Ted Mann, director:
Alan Taylor
03/04/2005 Complications
(Formerly 'Difficulties')
writer: Victoria Morrow,
director: Gregg Fienberg
10/04/2005 Something Very
Expensive
writer: Steve Shill, director:
Steve Shill
17/04/2005 E. B. Was Left Out
writer: Jody Worth, director:
Michael Almereyda
24/04/2005 Childish Things
writer: Regina Corrado,
director: Tim Van Patten
01/05/2005 Amalgamation
and Capital
writer: Elizabeth Sarnoff,
director: Ed Bianchi
08/05/2005 Advances, None
Miraculous
writer: Sara Hess, director:
Dan Minahan
15/05/2005 The Whores Can
Come
writer: Bryan McDonald,
director: Gregg Fienberg
22/05/2005 Boy-the- Earth-
Talks-To
writer: Ted Mann, director:
Ed Bianchi

Season Three
11/06/2006 Tell Your God to
Ready for Blood
writers: David Milch and Ted
Mann, director: Mark Tinker
18/06/2006 I Am Not The Fine
Man You Take Me For
writers: David Milch and
Regina Corrado, director:
Dan Attias
25/06/2006 True Colors
writers: Regina Corrado and Ted
Mann, director: Gregg Fienberg
02/07/2006 Full Faith and
Credit
writer: Ted Mann, director:
Ed Bianchi
09/07/2006 A Two-Headed
Beast
writer: David Milch, director:
Dan Minahan
16/07/2006 A Rich Find
writer: Alix Lambert, director:
Tim Hunter
23/07/2006 Unauthorized
Cinnamon
writer: Regina Corrado,
director: Mark Tinker
30/07/2006 Leviathan Smiles
writer: Kem Nunn, director:
Ed Bianchi
06/08/2006 Amateur Night
writers: Nick Towne and Zack
Whedon, director: Adam
Davidson
13/08/2006 A Constant Throb
writer: W. Earl Brown, director:
Mark Tinker
20/08/2006 The Catbird Seat
writer: Bernadette McNamara,
director: Gregg Fienberg
27/08/2006 Tell Him
Something Pretty
writer: Ted Mann, director:
Mark Tinker

Index

191

193